THE CAVALIER KING CHARLES SPANIEL

Myra Savant-Harris

The Cavalier King Charles Spaniel

Project Team
Editor: Mary E. Grangeia
Copy Editor: Joann Woy
Indexer: Elizabeth Walker
Designer: Stephanie Krautheim
Series Design: Stephanie Krautheim and Mada Design
Series Originator: Dominique De Vito

T.F.H. Publications
President/CEO: Glen S. Axelrod
Executive Vice President: Mark E. Johnson
Publisher: Christopher T. Reggio
Production Manager: Kathy Bontz

T.F.H. Publications, Inc.
One TFH Plaza
Third and Union Avenues
Neptune City, NJ 07753

Printed and bound in China
09 10 11 12 13 14   1 3 5 7 9 8 6 4 2

Library of Congress Cataloging-in-Publication Data
    Savant-Harris, Myra.
      The Cavalier King Charles spaniel / Myra Savant-Harris.
          p. cm.
      Includes index.
      ISBN 978-0-7938-3679-6 (alk. paper)
      1. Cavalier King Charles spaniel. I. Title.
      SF429.C36S38 2009
      636.752'4--dc22
                            2008046281

This book has been published with the intent to provide accurate and authoritative information in regard to the
subject matter within. While every reasonable precaution has been taken in preparation of this book, the author
and publisher expressly disclaim responsibility for any errors, omissions, or adverse effects arising from the use or
application of the information contained herein. The techniques and suggestions are used at the reader's discretion
and are not to be considered a substitute for veterinary care. If you suspect a medical problem consult your
veterinarian.

The Leader In Responsible Animal Care For Over 50 Years! ®
www.tfhpublications.com

TABLE OF CONTENTS

HISTORY

of the Cavalier King Charles Spaniel

I t is somewhat ironic that the Cavalier King Charles Spaniel, a dog of English origin, owes so much to an American gentleman named Mr. Roswell Eldridge, a dog fancier from Long Island, New York. Mr. Eldridge's interest was piqued upon seeing paintings dating from the 15th through the early part of the 19th century that depicted a small spaniel dog in a variety of settings. An artist named Pisanello painted such a canvas as early as 1440, and hundreds of other paintings by renowned European artists such as Vermeer, Van Dyke, Titian, Landseer, Stubbs, and Hogarth, also showed small spaniel dogs in family and sports settings, and in outdoor groupings. Once called "cocking spaniels," these little dogs were pictured very realistically, and as Mr. Eldridge noted, they were quite common during the reign of King Charles II (1660–1685). Centuries later, Queen Victoria, who was crowned in 1838, was shown with her little tricolor spaniel named Dash in several paintings by Landseer. So, from European artwork, we know that the charming little spaniel with the long ears and long muzzle was the companion of royalty from around 1440 until at least 1838, a period of almost 400 years.

When Mr. Eldridge visited England in 1925, he was surprised and dismayed to find that the little spaniel dog he had admired in the paintings was no longer in existence. It had been replaced by the King Charles Spaniel, a slightly smaller dog of the same four colors as the Cavalier King Charles Spaniel; although this dog was similar to the original little dog in coloration, it had a different head altogether. The little spaniel dog of King Charles' time had a longer face and muzzle, a shallow stop or no stop at all, and a flat skull, often with a spot in the center. The King Charles Spaniel, which was favored after about 1840, has a very flat face, a deep stop, and a domed skull.

Mr. Eldridge decided to offer dog breeders in England an incentive to recreate the small spaniel he had admired in European artwork. He arranged for a prize of £25 to be given at the 1926 Crufts Dog Show to both the dog and bitch that most closely resembled the small dog in Van Dyke's famous portrait "The Children of Charles I." This prize would be offered for three consecutive years.

EARLY DEVELOPMENT OF THE CAVALIER

It is uncertain exactly which dogs were used to recreate the little spaniel of King Charles' time. Most experts believe the King Charles Spaniel was used because it had a tendency to throw back to the longer muzzle and did so quite often. Cocker Spaniels are said to have been used, with Kennel Club (KC) approval, as late as the 1950s to improve Cavalier stock. Papillons were likely used perhaps to bring down the size. Crosses between some of these breeds and Welsh Springer Spaniels were used as well.

It is important to remember that when breeders are attempting to recreate a specific look, pedigree becomes less important than overall appearance. Parentage is not as important when, for example, striving to create a specific head type. Or if the desired look is finally achieved but the dog is too large, a smaller dog will then be used to bring size down while keeping the desirable characteristics. The little bitch who won the prize of £25 at Crufts in 1927 is listed as having an unknown sire and an unknown dam on her registration certificate. Her name was Waif Julia, and although her parentage is unknown, it is thought that she was a throwback from King Charles breeding stock. Her breeder's name was Mrs. H. Pitt, who was later to become very instrumental in the breeding of Cavalier King Charles Spaniels.

Amice Pitt worked tirelessly on behalf of Cavaliers, both to have them recognized as a breed early on and to ensure that the breed was established along appropriate lines. She bred Cavaliers for over 50 years, and together with Mr. Eldridge, is responsible for the breed we know today. Without either of these remarkable individuals, those of us who love and enjoy Cavaliers might not have our beloved dogs.

Nosey Spaniels

The earliest small spaniels showed an easily discernible muzzle length. By the late 1800s and early 1900s, these "nosey" little spaniels had been replaced by the flatter-faced variety called the King Charles Spaniel. The length of the muzzle was the most highly prized characteristic of the Cavalier's early breeding stock. Even today, the length of the muzzle is described very specifically in the breed standard.

BREED HISTORY IN ENGLAND

In 1928, the Cavalier King Charles Spaniel Club was established in the United Kingdom. The name "Cavalier King Charles Spaniel" was chosen because it was considered important to maintain the breed's association with the King Charles Spaniel and the close relationship between the two breeds. At the club's first meeting, the breed standard was drawn up, and it has remained almost unchanged since. The standard was based on a live specimen, a

Developed in Great Britain, toy spaniels were originally bred to be hunters.

Cavalier named Ann's Son, who was bred by Miss Mostyn Walker. The 1928 breed standard called for:

"an…active, sporting, fearless dog with a head that is almost flat between the ears, no dome desired. Dark, large and round eyes, but not prominent. Slight stop, about 1½ inches, black nose, muzzle pointed, coat, long and silky, all colours recognized. A moderate chest, ears to be long and feathered, high set, tail longish, docked, moderate bone on the legs with feet well feathered, weight 10 to 18 pounds. Faults, undershot and light eyes…."
—*The Cavalier King Charles Spaniel Club Millennium Year Book,* 2000

At that first meeting, reproductions of paintings showing the small spaniels of the 16th, 17th, and 18th century were on display and were also used to identify the characteristics that would identify breed type. From the very beginning, the club was adamant that "the dog should be guarded from fashion and there was to be no trimming. The perfectly natural dog was desired, and was not to be spoilt to suit individual tastes, or as the saying goes, carved into shape" (*The Cavalier King Charles Spaniel Club Millennium Year Book,* 2000). Even today, the efforts of many breeders encourage judges to avoid awarding wins to dogs who

A Regal Companion Pet

Small breeds of spaniel have been popular in Great Britain for many centuries. Although originally developed to be hunters, toy spaniels eventually became popular as companion pets. Some centuries later, they were especially revered as pets of the royal family. It was said that England's Mary Queen of Scots was beheaded with a black and tan spaniel under her skirts. Refusing to ever leave her side, he died from grief several days later. King Charles II, known as the "cavalier king," so adored his dogs that he decreed that they be allowed admittance to any public place, including the houses of Parliament. Modern-day Cavaliers are among the most popular toy breeds and are considered by many to be the ultimate lap dogs because of their highly affectionate, patient, and eager-to-please nature.

have been obviously trimmed or altered.

Ann's Son was the model of the Cavalier breed standard, and he is probably still found in the pedigrees and heritage of every Cavalier King Charles Spaniel today. He weighed only 13 pounds (6 kg), was short backed, and had a flat head. His muzzle was rather long, with no stop; his nose was black; and his eyes were large, round, and dark. He was a Blenheim, having a white background coat with rich chestnut brown markings. Said to have had a lovely temperament, he was described as an exquisite little dog with an enchanting personality. Ann's Son won at Crufts in 1928, 1929, and 1930. He was never defeated in his show career. Thanks to the earliest Cavaliers, Waif Julia and Ann's Son, these little dogs were on their way to becoming one of the most beloved breeds in England.

English Kennel Club Recognition

The newly established breed was in its infancy, and the club that had been formed to support it and further its interests was just beginning its work. The club held its first meeting in 1928. Although the Cavalier King Charles Spaniel Club approached the English KC for separate registration on several occasions, the KC would not recognize Cavaliers as a breed until 1945. Prior to that time, the dogs were shown under the auspices of a variety of canine societies such as the Ladies Kennel Association and several regional dog shows.

By 1939, World War II had already encompassed the European continent, eventually including the British Isles and bringing England into the war effort. The many hardships encountered during wartime reduced the activities of all dog breeders there as well as abroad. Harsh circumstances made it difficult to maintain dogs and breeding kennels. Kennel Club records show that only 60 Cavaliers were registered between 1940 and 1945. We can be grateful that the breeders of that era were able to maintain at least some breeding activity during that time.

Once the war was over, Europe began to return to the normal activities of peacetime, and dog breeders began to reestablish their breeds and breed clubs. At their first meeting following the war, only 14 members were present at the reestablished Cavalier King Charles Spaniel Club. Among these members was a young woman named Mrs. Kate Eldred. It was Kate's bitch, Belinda of Saxon who won the first bitch Challenge Certificate (CC) and Best in Show in England. Kate Eldred later moved to Canada and then to the United States, where she became an influential and much revered breeder of Cavalier King Charles Spaniels.

It was also during this time that the club decided it would once again approach the KC to request a registry separate from the "short-faced King Charles." Club members felt that Cavaliers could only progress if their registration was separate and if they were formally recognized as an individual breed. On December 5th, 1945, the KC agreed that the breed could be registered under the name "Cavalier Spaniels." Later, the club requested that the name

Although enormously popular in England, Cavaliers were not introduced into the United States until 1952.

be changed to "Cavalier King Charles Spaniels," and this request was granted.

BREED HISTORY IN THE UNITED STATES

In the 20 years that had passed since Mr. Roswell Eldridge first offered his incentive in the form of prize money in 1925, much progress was made through the hard work and dedication of a handful of Cavalier fanciers in the UK.

Although in England Cavaliers grew in popularity by leaps and bounds, they were not introduced into the United States until 1952, at which time Lady Forwood of England sent a little black and tan dog to her friend, Sally Brown, in Kentucky. The little dog's name was Mercury. Mercury was the sixth known Cavalier King Charles Spaniel to come to the United States. Although they are thought to have first been imported in the 1940s, Sally Brown started the Cavalier King Charles Spaniel Club of the United States (CKCSC USA) in 1954. It was at Sally's home that the very first Cavalier dog show was held in 1962. There were 35 dogs in the show, handled by 26 owner/exhibitors. At that time, Sally turned the presidency of CKCSC USA over to her sister-in-law, Trudy Brown. Trudy Brown was influential in the breed and in the club until the time of her death in 1983.

For over 50 years, CKCSC USA was the only registry for Cavalier King Charles Spaniels in the United States. This club held specialty shows, acted as a registering body, and created a stud book. The CKCSC USA applied for and received miscellaneous status with the American Kennel Club (AKC) in 1962. The club, often called the "Old Club" by members, adopted a code of ethics that became very important to the membership. This code was considered by many Cavalier fanciers to be something of a safeguard against widespread commercialization of the breed. Cavalier breeders in the United States have always feared that the popularity of their breed would lead to their exploitation, as had happened with many other breeds. After members of CKCSC USA participated in AKC-sponsored obedience trials, the club filed a number of applications with the AKC requesting full recognition, but they were denied. In 1992, the AKC invited CKCSC USA to be the parent club for Cavaliers, but by an overwhelming margin the CKCSC USA membership denied that request. Subsequently,

a small group of CKCSC USA members worked with the AKC to create the parent club for Cavaliers and requested recognition from them. This recognition was granted in 1995. This club is called the American Cavalier King Charles Spaniel Club (ACKCSC). Cavaliers went into AKC competition for the first time in 1996.

Both clubs still function within the United States. Many Cavalier fanciers choose to register their Cavaliers with both clubs, enjoying both the more exclusive and less frequent specialty shows offered by CKCSC USA, as well as the frequent all-breed AKC shows in their own regions. Cavalier fanciers from both clubs still fear that the breed's popularity will result in its commercialization and abuse both by backyard breeders and by puppy mills. In 1966, Amice Pitt wrote: "Cavaliers are going ahead by leaps and bounds, with larger registrations, more Challenge Certificates, and increased popularity. Unfortunately, with all this tremendous success the usual pitfalls of a popular breed have crept in: ambition, greed and a lack of idealism." For those of us who love and adore our little spaniels, we can have no greater regret than the realization that her words continue to come true more and more as each year passes.

The American Kennel Club

The American Kennel Club (AKC) maintains a very informative website at www. akc.org. Along with obtaining valuable information about your breed, you are able to order a copy of your dog's personal history and his five-generation pedigree. Pet owners often enjoy seeing the dogs in their pet's ancestry, and the format used is suitable for framing if desired.

INFLUENTIAL BREEDERS

No discussion of the Cavalier King Charles Spaniel would be complete without proper recognition of the people who have been influential to the breed. As discussed, England's Mrs. Amice Pitt must be at the top of any such list. Also included would be Sir Dudley and Lady Mary Forwood, Miss Mostyn Walker, Mrs. Jane Pitt, and Madame Trois Fontaines. Some of the later breeders who, together with their dogs, have influenced the future of Cavaliers are Mrs. Molly Coaker of Homerbrent Cavaliers, Mrs. Pam Thornhill of Kindrum Cavaliers, Gordon and Norma Inglis of Craigowl Cavaliers, Mrs. Sylvia Lymer of Lymrey Cavaliers, and Brian Rix and Kevan Berry of Ricksbury Cavaliers. These important UK breeders laid the foundation for the development of the Cavalier King Charles Spaniel both in England and in the United States. Mrs. Shealagh Waters of Maibee Cavaliers has been influential both in the United Kingdom and the United States, with the Maibee kennel name standing behind some of the more influential Cavaliers in both countries.

In the United States, Kate Eldred and her Turnworth Cavaliers have had a significant influence not only over the breed but the

Cavaliers have won many show championships, and it's easy to see why.

breeders who have been fortunate enough to work with her. She is widely respected and has mentored many newcomers. Mrs. Elizabeth Spalding was there at the beginning with her Kilspindie Cavaliers and has remained a positive influence for decades. C. Anne Robins of Chadwick Cavaliers and Pat Winters of Cobblestone Cavaliers, also important breeders in the United States, were at the very forefront of encouraging health testing. Annual cardiac checkups by a board-certified canine cardiologist were relatively unheard of at the time when both of these breeders campaigned tirelessly to encourage all US breeders to health-check their breeding stock and eliminate dogs who didn't pass their yearly exams from breeding programs. By 2006, this yearly cardiac exam was considered a routine part of breeding activities by most Cavalier breeders.

Mrs. Cathy Gish of Flying Colors Cavaliers also deserves a place as an influential breeder because of her many "firsts." At this time, she is the first and only breeder to have bred all four colors of Cavaliers and subsequently take them to their championships in the CKCSC USA. She was the first US breeder to win an AKC championship on all four colors as well. Her dog, AKC Champion Flying Colors Austin-Healey was the first American-bred Cavalier to travel to England and compete at the prestigious Crufts dog show.

Mr. and Mrs. Ted Eubanks of Pinecrest Cavaliers made their mark with their many home-bred champions, as did Mr. and Mrs. Harold Letterly with their beautiful boys, who are behind the pedigrees of many well-known show dogs. Mrs. Karin Ostmann of Sheeba Cavaliers is recognized for her many home-bred champions and particularly for being the breeder of the lovely tricolor boy, Sheeba Special Edition. To have been able to follow the show career of this remarkable dog has been a pleasure. In April of 1993, Sheeba Special Edition "James" was awarded Best Puppy in Sweeps at a CKCSC USA show. The judge was Joy Sims. Her comments about James were: "Special he was! Absolutely correct, movement to die for, and what a ring presence for one so young. He stole my heart. What a future he is going to have and—I want him!" He did indeed go on to have a stellar show career, and he sired many CKCSC USA and AKC champions. In 2004, true to Joy Sims prediction, James was ranked number one Cavalier stud dog in the US, having sired nine of the AKC champions of that year.

CHAMPIONS OF THE BREED

Show quality dogs have an opportunity to influence their breed in a positive manner in two different ways. Some of them influence the breed because their busy show careers allow many spectators to see what a beautifully built and constructed specimen of the breed is supposed to look like. Others influence the breed in the whelping nest, either as the dam or sire.

An example of how a Cavalier can influence the breed by what he produces is the lovely stud dog, AKC Champion Peakdowns Aidan, bred by Mr. and Mrs. Colin Turnbull of the United Kingdom and owned by Myra Savant-Harris. Aidan sired 12 AKC Champions and several Canadian Champions before he turned four years of age. He stamps his get with a specific little "Aidan look" in litter after litter. He is the very definition of the term "prepotent stud dog," as well as being a joy to own.

The beautiful Annatika Andreas is a perfect example of how a special little Cavalier can educate spectators and judges alike by showing beautiful conformation. Andy was bred in the UK by George and Jenny MacAlpine of Annatika Cavalier, but he later came to the United States to live with Dale Martin and Kim Murphy, his co-owners. Andy made his entrance into the AKC show ring at a time when American spectators and judges were just

beginning to see Cavaliers in the ring. Because they were relatively new, neither spectators nor judges really had the "eye" to assess them. Andy was, for Dale and Kim, a "once in a lifetime dog." During his show career, he won 12 all-breed Best in Shows. He also won Best of Breed at Westminster three years in a row and is still the only US Cavalier to have won both the AKC National Specialty and the CKCSC National Specialty. Andy was the epitome of the Cavalier breed standard, winning Best of Breed in show after show. It was a joy and a privilege for me to have known his breeder and his American co-owners and to watch him both at work and at play. What an education he gave us all.

In the United States, one can hardly discuss modern-day influential Cavaliers without going back to the pedigrees of their English ancestors. There are simply too many beautiful Cavaliers in the UK to name without running the risk of leaving some out: Mrs. Thornhill's lovely Alberto of Kindrum is in the pedigree of some of the loveliest dogs in both England and the States. His son,

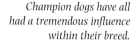

Champion dogs have all had a tremendous influence within their breed.

Famous Cavalier Owners

King Charles II was accused of "playing with his dogs all the time and not minding his business." Many modern-day Cavalier owners can well identify with him.

If you own a Cavalier, you are in good company. Other famous people who have owned Cavaliers include:

- Lauren Bacall
- Courtney Cox
- Terri Hatcher
- Jennifer Love Hewitt
- Brad Paisley
- Princess Margaret
- President Ronald Reagan
- Diane Sawyer
- Frank Sinatra
- Sylvester Stallone
- Liv Tyler

Linjato Ace of Base, sired many English Champions. "Dylan" as he is called, was bred by Linda Flynn. Caroline Ackroyd-Gibson was the breeder of Toraylac Joshua, who was well-known for producing wonderfully plush and full heads. His influence (and his head!) can still be seen in dogs today. Both Lymrey Royal Reflection and Lymrey Royal Scandal (litter brothers), who were bred by Sylvia Lymer, have had a wide reaching influence, both in the UK and the US. Royal Scandal sired Ricksbury Royal Legend, who won 33 Challenge Certificates and Best of Breed three times at Crufts. These dogs have all had tremendous influence within the breed, and it is with great pride that Cavalier owners worldwide can lay claim to having them in the pedigrees of their own Cavaliers.

Whether your Cavalier is your precious pet or a show dog who has filled your heart with pride, the breed's history is an interesting one. Cavaliers may be something of an engineered dog breed but if this is so, what a debt of gratitude we owe to the engineers.

CHARACTERISTICS

of the Cavalier King Charles Spaniel

Breeders create and maintain a breed by choosing animals that possess the traits needed to perform a specific function or set of functions. If you're looking for a pet, you may wonder why the original purpose of the breed matters to you; after all, you don't plan to ask your Cavalier to hunt or herd other animals. But it is important to understand the characteristics that make these dogs what they are because not every breed is right for every person. Let's take a look at the Cavalier breed standard to see the traits and talents for which it was developed.

THE BREED STANDARD

The official description of the way a particular dog should look and conduct himself is called the breed standard, and it is the ideal against which all dogs of that breed are measured. Show dogs in conformation are judged by how closely they compare to this "standard of perfection." Keep in mind, however, that the standard describes the ideal Cavalier; dogs who deviate from the standard still make wonderful pets.

General Description

Cavalier King Charles Spaniels are active, robust toy spaniels. They are well-balanced and sturdy, with a happy and free movement and a fearless and sporting character. Although they are in the toy dog category, they should have the graceful look and temperament of a little sporting dog in a lovely and elegant body. Cavaliers should never be shy or fearful of people or other animals. At the same time, they should be affectionate, gentle, and friendly to all. Temperament is as much a part of the breed standard for Cavaliers as is their size, color, and body shape. It is of utmost importance in this breed, and it is one of the characteristics that make them so very desirable as a companion pet.

Body

The height of the Cavalier taken at the shoulder is approximately 12 to 13 inches (30.5 to 33 cm). The measurement from the withers to the elbow is approximately the same as from the elbow to the floor. Cavaliers should not appear to be short in the leg, nor should they be leggy looking. The overall look should be well-balanced and graceful, and slightly longer than tall. They should not appear to be long and low, nor tall and leggy. They should have moderate bone, and should not appear to be weedy or coarse. Cavaliers should not look delicate or light in bone. They should have sufficient bone to look strong but graceful and energetic. Even small Cavaliers will be heavier in hand than they appear. The body should be short coupled with well-sprung ribs. The ribs should not give a "barreled" impression. The chest should be moderately deep, extending to the level of the elbows with plenty of room for the heart. The body should not have a tucked-up appearance at the loins.

Head

Cavalier King Charles Spaniels are said to be a "head" breed. That statement means that the look and character of the dog is often marked by the appearance of the head. Correct head type is essential to breed type.

The head should be in good proportion to the size of the body, not too large or too small. It should be slightly rounded but flat across the top. The long, well-set ears, luxuriously large and feathered, sit high on the head, framing the face. Above all else, the head and face must look gentle and soft. The expression is paramount and should be sweet and melting. Anyone who has ever had to refuse yet another doggy treat to a Cavalier is well familiar with the term "melting." Those large, round dark eyes with their charming expression can melt even the hardest of hearts.

There is a subtle difference between the heads of males (dogs) and females (bitches). The head of the dog is slightly wider and "heavier" looking. The bitch's head is more feminine and more defined. Although subtle, the differences will soon become apparent at a glance if you see enough Cavaliers.

Head Turners

Cavaliers are said to be a "head" breed, which means that a judge at a dog show will often place more weight on the beauty of the dog's head than on his tail set, gait, or other structural quality. A perfect head is proportionate to the size of the dog, appearing neither too small nor too large for the body. Having both the correct head and the perfect melting expression of the eyes gives the pleasing impression of beauty combined with sweetness, which is an important characteristic of the breed.

Eyes

Cavaliers should have large, rounded eyes that are neither bulging nor prominent. The color is dark, warm brown. Light brown or tan eyes are a fault and will be penalized by judges in competition. The rims of the eyes should be dark; the look is similar to that of eye liner or mascara on human eyes. The eyes are forward-looking with a trusting and gentle look. The whites of the eyes should not be noticeable. The melting expression is somewhat lessened if the white of the eye can be seen as a rim around the eye or if it is very noticeable in the inner corners of the eyes. It is highly desirable, although not a necessity, that the eyelid located in the innermost corner of the eye is also pigmented with a deep brown pigment. This decreases the visible white by a considerable amount. By looking into the eyes of the Cavalier King Charles Spaniel, you can see into the very soul of a dog who is trusting, loving, and fearless. Delightful dogs, they are as lovely on the inside as they are on the outside.

The Cavalier has soft brown eyes and long feathered ears.

Muzzle

The muzzle of the Cavalier King Charles Spaniel should be about 1.5 inches (3.8 cm) from the stop of the head to the tip of the nose. Muzzle length is an important characteristic that makes it easy to distinguish the Cavalier from the English Toy Spaniel. (This breed is called the Prince Charles in the United Kingdom.) The English Toy Spaniel has a very deep stop with a very short muzzle and an almost flat face. The muzzle of the Cavalier tapers gradually to give a clean finish to the face.

The length of the muzzle may differ slightly depending on the size of the dog, but the overall look should be well balanced. "Snipey" (long and thin) muzzles are as undesirable in the Cavalier as a flat face with no muzzle and prominent eyes. The muzzle should be well cushioned and padded with noticeable width. The nose should be jet black. Freckles, or "beauty marks," can be present on the muzzle, but they should not be located in the blaze between the eyes. It is not exactly a flaw, but it distracts from the melting expression of the dog.

Cavaliers should have a stop that is deeper and more pronounced than that of the Cocker Spaniel, but not as deep and pronounced as the English Toy Spaniel. (The stop is the area located directly between the eyes and on the top of the muzzle.) To get a feeling for what it is exactly, imagine placing a marble on top of the muzzle and between the eyes of the dog. A very deep stop would hold the marble securely in place, while a very shallow stop would allow the marble to roll off the end of the nose. Cocker Spaniels have a shallow stop, English Toy Spaniels have a very deep stop, and Cavalier King Charles Spaniels have a moderate stop at the top of a muzzle of moderate length.

The bite of a Cavalier is important, with a scissors bite being preferred; the upper teeth should overlap the lower teeth, and all of the teeth should be set squarely in the jaw. An imperfect bite does not affect the health of the dog except in very extreme circumstances. Bites that are imperfect are a frequent reason for breeders to place an otherwise lovely little puppy into a pet home. In competition, an overbite is a flaw, as is an underbite. However, a snipey muzzle with a perfect bite is less desirable than a slightly undershot mouth in an otherwise lovely face.

The neck of a Cavalier should be fairly long with a nice reach to it. It should be slightly crested and set nicely into gentle sloping

Measuring Up to the Standard

A breed standard describes what is considered to be perfection in the breed. It describes each part of the dog in great detail, including the coloring and personality, or temperament, of the dog. Very few dogs ever match the standard in every area, but having such a document gives breeders and exhibitors a target to shoot for when making choices that will ensure that Cavaliers will remain Cavaliers for generations to come.

shoulders. The overall look of the head and the slightly crested neck should be regal and graceful. The neck and shoulders should lead elegantly to a level topline. The topline should remain level when the dog is on the move, as well as when he is standing in a relaxed free "stack" or stance.

Tail

The tail of the Cavalier King Charles Spaniel should be well set and carried proudly and happily, but not carried up over the back or curled over the back like that of a Siberian Husky. The level of the tail should not be much higher than the topline and should be moving at all times while the dog is in motion. Occasionally, a breeder will exercise the option to dock the tail, but no more than one-third of the tail length should ever be removed. This does not appear to be done very often. The length of the tail should be in correct balance with the body of the dog. The "flag," or feathering, on the tail begins to appear in its most infantile form around the age of five to seven months, and on an adult dog it should be long and luxurious. The tail should be feathered generously with a long, silky coat.

Tail carriage can often be a tell-tale sign of the dog's temperament; it should never be carried between the legs or in a nervous manner. A male may carry his tale higher when he is around other males, or if he is around bitches in season, but the tail carriage should revert to approximately the level of the topline when the dog is on lead or when he is settled.

Forequarters

The Cavalier's shoulders should be well laid back. The neck, with its slightly muscled crest and reach, should work harmoniously with the well-laid back shoulders to give the dog an elegant look while in motion.

The front legs should be straight and tucked well under the body, with the elbows close in to the sides. The pasterns should be strong, with compact feet and well-cushioned paws. The dewclaws may be removed on both front and rear feet. They are located in close proximity to what would be the thumb on the human hand. They do not serve a known purpose and are easily removed when the puppies are about three days old. This is a breeder's option. Cavaliers are only occasionally born with dewclaws on the hind

The Cavalier is a toy breed, meaning that it is proportionately small.

feet, but they are all born with them on the front feet.

Hindquarters

The hindquarters of the Cavalier should be well constructed, coming down from a broad pelvis that is moderately muscled. The stifles should have a nice turn to them, and the hocks should be short and well let down. The hind legs, when viewed from the rear of the dog, should be parallel to each other. These nicely turned stifles, together with the shortened hocks, allow for a rear end movement that is very free-moving and graceful. Together with the appropriate tail set, this gives the Cavalier in motion his characteristic elegant yet athletic movement.

Coat

The coat of the Cavalier King Charles Spaniel is one of his most distinguishing features. It should be silky, straight, and of moderate length. Slight waving is permissible and is frequently noted on the hindquarters of the dog. Feathering on the ears, chest ("bib"), legs, and tail should be long. Feathering over the feet, forming the "slippers," is a particular feature of the breed.

No trimming of the coat is permitted. Judges are encouraged to penalize or eliminate from competition any specimens of the breed who are obviously altered by scissors, clippers, bleaching, or dying. Hair growing between the pads on the underside of the feet may be trimmed as part of the regular maintenance of the feet. Of course, pet owners are allowed to trim their pets as desired; the rules concerning coat trimming are applicable only to show dogs competing in the show ring.

Colors

Cavaliers come in four colors: Blenheim, tricolor, black and tan, and ruby. The most common is Blenheim, which gets its name from the estate of the Duke of Marlborough in the United Kingdom. The Duke's dogs, who were chestnut and white, were much desired for hunting; hence, this color pattern was named after them.

Blenheim

Blenheims have a white background with rich chestnut brown markings. The richer, deeper reds on the Cavalier coat are very desirable. Lighter shades of brown are not as desirable but are not a disqualification in the show ring. The white should be pearly, clean, and free of ticking. Ticking refers to many spots of a darker color within a body of white. Freckles are occasional spots that may be on the face, legs, or feet. In other words, freckles refer to a few spots while ticking refers to many.

The ears of the Blenheim are brown, and the color is evenly spaced on the head and surrounding both eyes. It is not unusual for the brown on the ears and feathering to be slightly lighter in color than the brown on the coat. This is not a fault and is simply a function of the age of the hair itself. The hair on the body sheds more often and is replaced more frequently than that of the longer feathering on the ears and tail. As the hair ages, it lightens in color due to exposure to sunlight or shampoos.

The white blaze on the face is between the eyes and ears. Some Cavaliers are born with a spot of color, or "Blenheim spot," in the center of the blaze. Also called a lozenge, this spot is very unique looking and desirable, but it is not a necessary breed characteristic. It is desirable for the chestnut markings on the head to be symmetrical, but it is not essential for the show dog to exhibit symmetrical markings.

"Ideal" or perfect markings consist of chestnut covering 50 percent to 60 percent of the dog and white covering the remaining

Lucky Markings

Cavaliers have traditionally been thought to have "lucky" markings. The term originated when an early breeder, Amice Pitt, referred to the "lucky" elbow on parti-colored Cavaliers. This lucky elbow can best be described as an area of color extending over the elbows on both front legs. The markings are probably considered to be "lucky" because at some point in the early show history of the breed, some of the dogs who were winning awards possessed them. Nowadays, they are rarely noticed and never discussed.

The silky, feathered coat of the Cavalier King Charles Spaniel is one of his most distinguishing features.

40 percent to 50 percent. The term "heavily marked" refers to a dog with much more chestnut than white. The term "lightly marked" refers to a dog with much more white than chestnut. While markings must be clean and well defined from the white, more lightly and heavily marked dogs are often correct and competitive in the show ring.

Tricolor

Tricolor is the second most common coloration of the Cavalier King Charles Spaniel. Tricolor Cavaliers have shiny black markings on a pearly white background. The black coat should be free of a "rusty" look and have a deep black appearance. The white should be pearly, clean looking, and free of excessive ticking. The eyebrows, inner aspect of the ears, and the area under the base of the tail should be a bright, coppery tan. Both eyes must be surrounded by black. The ears must be black. The white blaze will very occasionally contain a black lozenge, which is especially treasured because of its rarity but certainly not an essential characteristic of the breed. The lozenge on either a Blenheim or a tricolor is simply frosting on an otherwise delightful little cake.

Black and Tan

Cavaliers come in two whole-color shades: black and tan and ruby. The black and tan is primarily a rich, shiny black with rich coppery tan "points" over the eyebrows, under both ears, and under the base of the tail. The rich tan fur under both ears will often curl winningly over the front of the ears and frame the face with the two lovely colors of the dog. The black on the coat should be clear and clean.

Ruby

Ruby Cavaliers are very striking. The chestnut pigment covers the entire body. On the feathering of ears and tail, it may be lighter in color. This is not considered to be a flaw as it may occur with aging. The overall coloration on the ruby should be a rich, deep red.

Aging and Changes in Coloration

Blenheim and ruby puppies are born with lighter colored fur on their chestnut markings. This lighter color is lost when the puppy coat sheds and is replaced by deeper, richer colored hair as the puppy matures.

Tricolors and black and tans (which are particolors—a predominant color broken by patches of one or more other colors) are born a deep, shiny black color that they will always maintain. As the puppy grows older, the darkest color of the particolor coat seems to grow more dominant while the white appears to decrease in size. Be mindful of this fact if you plan to purchase a show dog. A very narrow white blaze on a puppy will most likely disappear entirely on the adult dog. Very small areas of white surrounded by the darker color may very well not be visible on the adult dog as well.

There is no preferred color in Cavaliers. Dogs of all four colors will exhibit all of the characteristics of the breed.

Gait

The Cavalier's gait is free moving and elegant. The dog should have good reach in the front end and a sound, driving rear action. When viewed from the side, his movement should show a good length of stride, with the topline staying flat. When viewed from the front or back (coming or going), the dog should go straight and true, which is the result of a well-made front end and free-moving, sound construction in the rear. When coming toward you, the dog should not appear to be elbowing out, and when viewed while going away, the hocks should stay parallel and not shift toward the midline.

The Cavalier should not have a paddling, hackneyed gait. A hackneyed gait is a movement that causes the front paws to lift up slightly and the bottom of the feet to flash as the dog goes along. In Cavaliers, this gait is usually a result of a shorter than acceptable upper arm, sometimes coupled with a shorter than acceptable neck. Often a dog who "paddles" will be slightly high in the rear because he is slightly short in the front end. Unfortunately, a hackneyed gait can be rather flashy looking unless you are able to accurately visualize the structural flaw that has produced it. The appropriate gate for the show Cavalier on a loose lead is moderately fast, with the spirit necessary to convey the correct, gay temperament that is a necessary part of the breed's character.

In competition, the Cavalier should be moving out slightly ahead of the handler, with the lead loosely hanging between the two of them. Cavaliers should never be held up tightly by the neck. The action of "stringing" up the neck will accentuate any structural flaws of the front end. It is part of the breed standard that they must be handled gently, allowed to move on a loose lead, and allowed to greet the judge if they please. It is a pleasure to watch a well-trained Cavalier in the show ring, moving along freely, full of life and joy, with the tail in constant motion and conveying his happiness to all who are watching.

If you think you would like to participate in competition, the best way to learn about good structure and correct ring behavior is to attend dog shows and sit ringside watching the exhibits. Take notes on what you see. Watch how the dogs are handled. Try to guess which dog the judge will put up for the points that day. Over time, you will learn about appropriate temperament in the show ring. Don't expect to learn everything in a day, a week, or even a year. In the same way that it takes years of practice to coordinate a musical education by learning melody, harmony, timing, and beauty, it will take years of practice to understand and coordinate structure, markings, movement, and ring "presence." Your dog show eye will develop with experience.

TEMPERAMENT AND PERSONALITY

Cavalier King Charles Spaniels are friendly and gay, with no tendency toward nervous or shy behaviors. Their temperament is generally fearless and outgoing. Bad temper, as exhibited by growling or aggressive behaviors, is not tolerated and can exclude the dog from competition. Shyness is also not a desirable characteristic of the breed. Shyness does not refer to puppies who have not yet learned their way around the neighborhood, but refers instead to obvious mistrust and fearfulness in an adult dog. As the American Kennel Club (AKC) breed standard states, "fearlessness is not meant to suggest the fearlessness of a warrior, but that of an innocent who cannot imagine any harm coming to it, thereby inspired to confidence and trustfulness." Often a breeder will place puppies who exhibit shy, soft tendencies in a pet home. These animals make lovely pets and will often come out of their shell when in a loving home.

Cavalier King Charles Spaniels are, without a doubt, the most versatile of all dogs, a characteristic that makes them very desirable. Despite being small, they are robust, athletic, and energetic. With an ideal body weight of 13 to 18 pounds (5.9 to 8.2 kg), they are easily portable, but still large enough to have plenty of stamina to enjoy almost any activity. Although they are classified as toy dogs, they are not in the least bit fragile. They are the largest of the toy group, and it's not unusual to find one who weighs 9 or 10 pounds (4.1 or 4.5 kg) or as much as 24 pounds (11 kg) or so. Remember that the weight shown in the breed standard is really the ideal for showing, but some leniency is given for well-balanced Cavaliers whose weight exceeds the breed standard. While it's unusual to find a Cavalier who weighs less than the standard ideal in the show ring, it is common to find one who exceeds it.

Love Sponges

The most beloved characteristic of Cavaliers is their sweet, kissable, and delightful temperament. Even avowed "dog haters" find themselves drawn into the web of love and affection that is effortlessly woven by them. Extremely social, most dogs of the breed are playful, extremely patient, and eager to please.

Cavaliers are great with people of all ages, from children to seniors, which is just part of what makes them a very versatile dog. Requiring almost constant companionship from humans or other dogs, however, they are not suited to spending long periods of time on their own. Although their favorite choice of animal companions is another Cavalier, they will bond quite nicely to a family cat.

Cavaliers need exercise and relish it. Although they are happy to be indoor dogs, they are able to withstand and enjoy periods of play in almost any kind of weather.

The Cavalier's small size and strong body makes him perfect for most families because they are large enough to have stamina and strength, but small enough to be very portable without being delicate or easily injured.

Indoor/Outdoor Types

Because Cavalier King Charles Spaniels have a full coat that is silky and lush, with ample feathering on the ears and limbs, they are not subject to the cold stress that many shorter haired dogs face. They love being outdoors, but only with their owners and loved ones. Cavaliers enjoy daily walks, particularly if they are able to meet and greet passersby. They do not particularly enjoy getting rained on, though, so many appreciate having an umbrella held over them or the comfort of wearing a little rain jacket.

Cavaliers need exercise and relish it, but their daily pleasure is as much based on frequent socialization as it is on athletic endeavors. These endearing little dogs want nothing more than to be with people, and they enjoy making new acquaintances.

Universally well known to be heedless in their pursuit of anything that catches their fancy, Cavaliers must be protected when out of the home. For example, they won't hesitate in the least to run across the road in pursuit of a butterfly or to greet an old friend.

When out and about with your Cavalier, he is best kept on lead at all times. The use of extra long, flexible leads are not recommended when wandering on or near roadways. Never allow your Cavalier to walk off lead except in completely fenced and protected areas.

Although Cavaliers are definitely happy to be indoor dogs, they are able to withstand and indeed enjoy periods of play in almost any kind of weather. They love a good long romp in the snow, and will exhibit their exuberant natures as they are dashing about in drifts. Even a young pup will enjoy a brief run through the snowfall, chasing after snowflakes, as long as he can be warmed up in front of a roaring fireplace afterward.

Being spaniels, Cavaliers also tend to enjoy water sports. Many will jump right into a pool or river. Sometimes, they are not particularly cautious. It is typical of their nature to rush headlong into any activity that looks like fun without worrying about the dangers involved. They enjoy running on the beach, chasing shore birds, and boating activities. They are good swimmers, and like all dogs, they do not need to be taught to swim. Their versatility, love of play, and constant desire to spend time with their families make them ideal companions.

Compatibility With Other Dogs

Taking a Cavalier to a dog park can be a fun activity; watching him interact with other small dogs can be quite enjoyable. Interestingly, Cavaliers are well known to have a certain preference for other members of their own breed, especially those of their own color: Blenheims will gravitate toward other Blenheims and tricolors will head toward other tricolors and so on. By watching how keen a Cavalier is on joining another Cavalier of his coloration, you can clearly see that not only can they see colors, but they are aware of the color of their own coat as well. They are positively exuberant when allowed to romp and play with one of their own.

That being said, precautions must be taken when Cavaliers interact with larger and potentially more aggressive dogs. Studies have been done demonstrating that Cavaliers show the least amount of wolf-like tendencies, while breeds such as Siberian Huskies, Akitas, and Malamutes demonstrate the most wolf-like tendencies. Cavaliers are actually more childlike than doglike. They do not speak "dog," the instinctive canine language that

Cavaliers tend to adjust well to other pets—even cats.

has evolved over generations. They don't raise their hackles, hold their ears back, or crouch to demonstrate their anger, nor do they bare their teeth. Cavaliers don't always know how to interpret the unspoken "language" of other dogs and may not understand that ears held back or bared teeth are warning signals. To the contrary, a Cavalier interprets any look in his general direction as an open invitation to play. As a result, he may bound heedlessly forward hoping to make friends with an aggressive dog. But an aggressive or agitated dog, particularly a much larger one, presents a very real threat and could, if provoked, harm or kill him.

When taking your Cavalier out, especially to a dog park, you must be sure that the other animals within the area are safe and well controlled before allowing him to run off lead. If you walk your Cavalier in your neighborhood or in an area frequented by other dog walkers, you must exercise caution when approaching larger dogs until you have made sure that the unfamiliar dog can safely interact with your dog. For reasons of safety, pick up your Cavalier until larger dogs have passed by you. Again, flexible leads are not a good choice unless the area is secured, safe, and free from both potentially dangerous dogs and automobiles.

Country or City?

Cavaliers do well in any environment that can be secured for their safety. They do well in apartments as long as they can be regularly walked and exercised. Their small size makes them ideal pets for the apartment dweller. Usually very quiet and mild mannered, Cavaliers are not prone to barking a lot. They may let you know if they hear a door bell ringing, and they are sure to bark if they hear someone knocking on the door. Interpret this not as a warning to you, but as the excited realization that company is coming to play with and pay attention to them. However, they cannot be counted on to raise the alarm if a burglar enters their home. To the contrary, if the burglar is sweet to your dog and tosses him a treat of some kind, he will probably happily leave home to go along with him on his next robbery. If you are looking for a guard dog, there are undoubtedly better choices than a Cavalier. It is the rare Cavalier who pines away for his owner if he is, of necessity, separated from him. It is part of the breed's charm and desirability that they find happiness with anyone who loves them, and they willingly share their love and affection with all.

Cavaliers also do well in a suburban setting. They enjoy having a yard for running about and chasing after balls. But you cannot plan to leave them outdoors on their own for very long without expecting to have a very unhappy little dog on your hands. Although they love all activities they share with their families, their expectation is that they will return home with you when playtime in the yard is over. They will tire of the outdoors quickly in your absence. Indoors, Cavaliers love an undraped window with a window seat. They enjoy watching what's going on in the neighborhood: cars going by, birds flying in the sky, and children at play. They become well-known and well-loved fixtures of a busy community.

Being versatile, Cavaliers can do well in a rural home environment as well. Again, you must take the precaution of securely fencing in an area specifically for your dog because he will think nothing of chasing butterflies and birds into the next field, and he will undoubtedly bark at new and larger farm animals until he gets to know them and settles into a rural atmosphere.

Cavaliers and Kids

Peanut butter and jelly, apples and cheese, dogs and children; some things are just made for each other. And you simply can't beat a Cavalier when it comes to teaming up a pet with a child. Sturdy enough to play outdoors for hours, attentive enough to watch television, and patient enough to wait for their child to return home from school, a Cavalier makes a wonderful and loving playmate.

Cavaliers do extremely well with children.

Cavaliers have a temperament somewhat similar to that of Golden Retrievers, but they have the delightfully small and portable body of a toy dog.

Cavaliers and Children

Cavaliers do extremely well with children. Although they are perfectly content to share a home with a single adult or to live with people who have no children, make no mistake about it: Cavaliers and children go together like coffee and cream.

Cavalier puppies are usually quite hardy, but nevertheless should be handled gently. A child who is going to be allowed to play with a puppy should be taught how to properly interact with one well before being introduced to him. Children need to be taught to sit calmly and allow a puppy to approach them first. They should be discouraged from chasing the puppy, because it will lead to undesirable behaviors in both the child and the dog. It's easier to teach a child appropriate behavior than it is to train a puppy in early "puppyhood," so this responsibility rests mainly with the child and not solely with the puppy. Children can easily be taught to sit while playing with a puppy rather than carrying a puppy around and putting him at risk for injury if he should fall or jump out of a child's arms.

All puppies love to snuggle and sit in your lap. They love to cuddle in the arms of a child and watch television; Cavaliers are avid television watchers! Once a puppy is a bit older, he and his pal can play together outdoors. Most children love to take their dog on walks in the neighborhood and can safely do so if they are taught the necessity to stay away from larger and potentially aggressive dogs. Cavaliers love children, and everyone loves a Cavalier.

Cavaliers, with their compact but energetic and robust little bodies, make lovely family pets, whether you are a family of one or have a large family filled with children. They do wonderfully well as show dogs, agility dogs, obedience dogs, therapy dogs, and as 4H dogs for children. They make lovely companions whether your lifestyle is active and athletic or if you are a couch potato seeking a companion for a night in front of the television. They thrive on small amounts of activity, but love longer exercise sessions and can easily occupy themselves for a time if you are busy. They do well on long walks, car trips, and shopping trips. They love water sports, but can entertain themselves for hours with a puddle of water while you garden. They function well within a household that has other pets. They don't require long hours of trimming, cutting, and sculpting, nor do they require rigorous training for the show ring. All this, and they require nothing in return for undying love and affection but good food, occasional exercise, and the opportunity to spend time with their owners.

PREPARING

for Your Cavalier King Charles Spaniel

Once you have decided that you want to share your life with Cavalier, you will need to make many decisions to find the right dog for you and to ensure that you have everything you need to get off to a great start. You'll also have to make appropriate preparations for his arrival. By planning ahead, you can have everything set up and ready for your new family member so that his transition into an unfamiliar place is a safe and stress-free experience.

INITIAL CONSIDERATIONS

One of the first choices you'll make in selecting your dog will involve the gender, color, and age you prefer.

Male or Female?

Do you want a male or a female? Try not to have a strong preference for gender, but instead let the puppies help you to make your decision. By keeping an open mind, you leave yourself open to options that will be more important in the long run to you than gender. If you are planning to own a pet-quality dog instead of a show dog, the puppy will most likely be neutered or spayed, so gender becomes much less of an issue.

Cavaliers do not exhibit the marked gender differences that are obvious in many other breeds. You will find Cavalier males to be every bit as loving and affectionate as females, perhaps even more so. That is part of what makes the breed so winning and so delightful. They love you no matter what their gender or age.

All Cavalier breeders agree that while your girls love you very much, your Cavalier boys fall "in love" with you. All Cavaliers make delightful companions and will be wonderfully devoted and affection pets for you and for your entire family.

Which Color?

What about color? Do you prefer the beautiful Blenheim, with his lovely pearly white and chestnut coat, or is the tricolor more appealing, with his striking white and glistening black coat? Perhaps the whole-color Cavalier makes your heart beat fast. The beauty of a perfectly turned out black and tan or the rich coppery tones of a ruby are simply not to be denied.

Dogs of each color have their own band of devotees, and each has their own brand of Cavalier perfection. Again, try to keep your options open if possible, but if you have made up your mind that you simply must own a Cavalier of a specific color, then once you begin your search for a puppy or adult in earnest, let color be your starting point. Many breeders only breed either particolors or whole colors, so it may take a while for you to find a breeder who specializes in the color of your choice.

Puppy or Adult?

A puppy comes with all the joys and pleasures of bringing home a new baby. There is the excitement and anticipation of his arrival, and then the thrill of that first little puppy kiss. Yet making a puppy part of your family presents its own unique challenges. Puppies require a large commitment of time and energy. At first, there will be significant day care needs because you won't be able to leave a youngster home alone during the day for long periods of time. Your puppy will require housetraining and obedience training, and you will also have to be prepared for teething, pet proofing, and all the other little mishaps that may occur as he makes a transition from littermate to independent pet. The puppy will just be starting to learn the language of humans versus dogs and will need patience and love from the entire family. Although this may seem like a lot of work, the positive aspect of this is that your puppy hasn't learned any bad habits—he's like a clean slate, and you get to establish the boundaries for his life with you so that you can live together in harmony.

If you prefer an adult, chances are good that you can find one, but it may take slightly longer. Often breeders will rehome a dog or bitch who has finished his or her show or breeding career. Breeders have limited space in their homes, and so as the dogs finish the jobs they've done with the breeder, the decision is frequently made to allow them to move on to a life of being as spoiled and pampered as every Cavalier should be.

Cavaliers are such loving, friendly dogs that they are truly

Deciding whether you want to get a puppy or adult Cavalier is an important decision.

happy being with anyone who loves them back. A Cavalier won't pine away for his former home or owner. Once you bring him home and introduce him to his new surroundings, he will settle in quickly. In a day or so, you'll feel as though you've had him forever.

An adult Cavalier may or may not be housetrained. Often, breeding stock doesn't have access to the entire house, so you may have to housetrain and obedience train such a dog. There are many advantages to purchasing an older dog, just as there are advantages to owning a puppy. The choice is yours to make based on your financial situation, your family needs, and your wishes and desires for your new Cavalier.

Whether you choose a little puppy, a teenager, or an adult, the pleasure of owning a Cavalier is the same regardless of age.

FINDING THE CAVALIER OF YOUR DREAMS

So, you've pretty much decided what you want in your Cavalier, but where do you go to find him? Dogs come into our lives in different ways. Sometimes dogs even find us. Either way, it's imperative to know what you're getting.

There are a number of ways to search for a pet. If you want a purebred dog, such as a Cavalier, your best bet is finding a breeder.

Breeder Checklist

Before you acquire your Cavalier, be sure to do your homework. It is beneficial for both you and your breeder to learn more about each other before you make decisions or sign an agreement on a dog of your choice.

A good breeder will let you visit and spend some time at her facility. She will guarantee that your puppy is in good health and free from illnesses. She will also require that you have your puppy neutered or spayed at the appropriate age, unless you have a show contract. Always demand a written sales agreement that describes all terms of the sale, including the breeder's health guarantee and the neuter/spay agreement.

Here are some basics to consider when evaluating a breeder:

- You may consider it an invasion of privacy, but a good breeder will not just dump a puppy in your arms and take a check. She'll ask you many questions about your home situation and may even want to speak with your veterinarian. Although these procedures can seem intrusive, a good breeder is looking out for the welfare of her dogs.

- A good breeder has a spotless kennel. The animals should appear clean, healthy, and well cared for, and they should be housed in clean, roomy kennels with fresh food and water.

- A good breeder will offer you a contract that clearly outlines your responsibilities in regard to the dog you are purchasing. Be sure to read it carefully and question anything you don't understand before signing it.

- A good breeder has a warm and chummy relationship with her dogs. It's very important that young dogs be introduced to the kind of life and circumstances they will be expected to live in by the time they are separated from their mom and littermates.

- A good breeder will happily provide references from former buyers.

- A good breeder is knowledgeable about the positives and negatives of her breed (no breed is perfect). She also may show her dogs.

- A responsible breeder will have had her dogs tested for certain genetic problems and inherited diseases. She will show you proof that your dog has passed these tests.

You can also inquire at breed rescue or adoption agencies; these are lovely dogs who may have been given up by families who could no longer keep them. Responsible ownership requires education, compassion, patience, and material resources. Start this experience right by finding the best way to bring a Cavalier into your life.

Breeders

Start searching for your Cavalier by interviewing breeders who are affiliated with Cavalier dog clubs. You can find those located within your geographical region by going to the Cavalier King Charles Spaniel Club—USA website at www.ckcsc.org or to the American Kennel Club (AKC) website at www.americankennelclub.org.

To purchase a Cavalier puppy from a reputable breeder, you may have to go outside of your immediate area, so be willing to look farther away from home. By beginning your search using the breeders listed, you'll speak with individuals actively showing their dogs and who are familiar with the breed standard. Also, because breeders are a tightly knit community, they can usually give you referrals if they do not have the puppy or dog that you are hoping to find. You can contact them by e-mail or phone to discuss what you are looking for and see what dogs they have available.

A breeder's puppies should look clean and healthy.

A show-quality Cavalier will have different physical attributes than a pet-quality Cavalier, but both can be wonderful companions.

Be advised that it is not considered proper etiquette to immediately ask about price. Breeders are focused on finding good homes for their puppies and in mentoring you as a new Cavalier parent, and they appreciate the same responsible attitude in prospective owners as well.

By purchasing a puppy from a reputable breeder when at all possible, you are taking advantage of his expertise and knowledge of Cavaliers and his long-time commitment to the breed. Breeders who also show their dogs work hard to see that their breeding program adheres as closely as possible to the standard of perfection for the breed. They have made serious efforts to ensure that their puppies will be of the correct size and type, and have religiously tested their breeding animals for genetically transmitted diseases. They are sometimes able to take advantage of health testing on the show grounds, which is often subsidized by the kennel club hosting the show. Because testing can be very expensive, breeders avail themselves of this opportunity whenever it's offered.

Visiting Kennel Facilities

Once you have selected and interviewed those breeders you are interested in, schedule an appointment to visit their kennels.

Observe all of the courtesies that would be applicable to any other business appointment. If you are unable to make your scheduled appointment, call ahead to cancel. While you may be embarrassed to admit that you purchased the first puppy you saw, other breeders on your list will appreciate being notified that you are not coming so that they don't spend a day at home needlessly awaiting your arrival. Don't worry too much about telling them that you have already purchased a puppy. They are used to it because they know better than anyone else that any Cavalier puppy is simply irresistible.

Be on time for your appointment. Don't bring a crowd along. Your goal is to see the puppy in as natural an environment as possible, and if you bring mom and dad, the in-laws, and others, you will most likely see puppies that are overly excited and confused. You will not have the opportunity to quietly discuss the puppy with the breeder. For the first visit, don't bring small children. They have a difficult time understanding why you are walking to the car and leaving behind the puppy with which they have just fallen in love. View this first visit to the breeder as your chance to have the undivided attention of both the dog and breeder, and give the breeder your undivided attention as well.

What to Expect

When you arrive at a breeder's kennel, you may be asked to remove your shoes or allow the breeder to spray a parvicide on them. You will be asked if you have visited a vet's office that day or if you have visited other kennels. The breeder is very keen on protecting her dogs from microorganisms that could feasibly be carried in on your clothing and shoes. She may ask you to sit for awhile and chat so that you can all begin to get to know one another. She will be interested to know what your home situation is: house or apartment, children, other animals. Cavalier breeders are protective not only of their particular puppies but of the breed in general. A fenced yard will be of great interest to a breeder who is preparing to sell you a puppy. If your stated intention was to purchase a pet and not a dog for breeding, you should be prepared to sign a contract agreeing to spay or neuter your pet. A reputable breeder will not sell a pet-quality puppy to you and then allow you to use him for breeding. There are valid reasons why a puppy is categorized "pet quality" or "show quality."

Pet Quality versus Show Quality

As the breeder rears her puppies, assessments are made from time to time to determine if any individuals are suitable for the show ring. A Cavalier puppy may be judged to be of pet quality at birth simply by virtue of his markings. Conversely, if a puppy is too heavily marked or too lightly marked, the breeder may decide that the markings will keep him from showing. A puppy who does not meet the breed standard by way of a specified fault will also be sold as a pet, for example one whose bite isn't perfect enough for the show ring. The placement of a shoulder or the anatomical features of the rear assembly are other types of considerations. These kinds of things are usually fairly insignificant or not even visible to a person looking for a pet to love, but to a breeder they forecast an animal's show potential. If you are curious, you can ask the breeder why the puppy is being sold as a pet, and she will often show or tell you the minor characteristic that helped her in arriving at that decision.

No matter where you decide to get your Cavalier, do your homework to make sure you choose the right dog for you and your family.

Paperwork

You can expect to be given a variety of paperwork when you purchase your dog. The breeder may insist on having you sign a written contract that requires you to agree to certain terms and to return the dog if you find yourself unable to keep him. While this request may seem unreasonable at first glance, it is actually a safeguard against the dog's future abuse. No breeder wants to think that a puppy she has carefully and lovingly placed ends up tied to a tree day and night. She would much rather take him back and rehome him.

Many reputable breeders include health guarantees as well. These guarantees may cover only general illnesses and be in effect for a brief period of time, or they may cover genetically transmitted diseases and be in effect for the life of the dog.

Read the contract carefully, and ask the breeder any questions you may have. You will most likely not receive the registration papers the day that you take your puppy home. The breeder may provide you with the information and forms necessary to join a chapter of a Cavalier club in your area. Many pet owners belong to such breed clubs, and they offer valuable resources to them. Also, just because you have chosen not to exhibit your dog does not mean you do not have a place within a dog club. Dues are usually nominal, and the meetings are generally only held once a month. Several pet-friendly activities are scheduled each year. These events are fun for the entire family and are wonderful ways to bond with your dog.

Health Records

Your breeder will provide you with health records for your puppy that list the dates he was immunized and dewormed, along with information about the deworming preparations and immunizations that were given. Some breeders also provide copies of health clearances on the parents. If not, you can ask for them. Your breeder might well recommend vets in your area who are familiar with Cavaliers and their specific needs.

Care Information

You should expect to be given instructions for the proper care and feeding of your new puppy or adult dog. These instructions should include grooming of the eyes, ears, feet, and coat. If you are unsure about any of these procedures, such as how to trim the dog's nails, asking the breeder for advice now will save you anxiety later on. Working with a professional breeder gives you the added advantage of having a mentor, someone you can trust, who will answer your questions over the next several weeks and possibly the next several years. Breeders specialize in guiding people who are new to the breed and are happy to do so.

The breeder should also provide you with the name and type of food that your new dog is used to eating and give you a small amount to take home. If you've had experience with dogs in the past, you may have fed a different type of food. Ask your breeder about her food preferences. If you decide to change the puppy's diet, it will be necessary to do so gradually.

Adoption Options

If you can't afford to pay the price for a professionally-bred Cavalier, why not adopt from a rescue group or shelter? You and the dog you adopt will both win, and you won't support irresponsible breeding. Fine adult Cavaliers needing good homes can always be found. Rescue groups often specialize in specific breeds, and it is sometimes possible to adopt from shelters.

Rescue Programs

If you decide to utilize Cavalier rescue groups to find your new pet, you may be put on a waiting list. Some report a wait as long as three years before placement. Unlike other popular breeds, Cavalier rescue groups do not receive large numbers of dogs into their programs each year. Those who do come into rescue are generally, although not always, older and displaced because of health reasons. It is certainly an option, and a noble one, but not for anyone who is seeking an instant response to their desire for a Cavalier.

Choosing a Healthy Puppy

A healthy 7- to 12-week-old puppy:

- is solid and well proportioned
- is neither too thin nor potbellied
- has soft, glossy fur
- has no red, itchy, or bald spots, and no fleas
- has a clean anal area
- has bright, clear eyes
- has pink gums and healthy breath (smelling only of the slightly musky odor of "puppy breath")
- has a correct bite and properly aligned jaws
- has a clean, damp nose, with no sign of discharge
- breathes without sneezing, coughing, or wheezing
- has clean ears
- moves well, with no signs of lameness or other problems
- is happy and playful

Shelters

Rescue groups try to monitor shelters so that they can find Cavaliers prior to their placement. They will also attempt to locate the dog's original breeder. Quite often, breeders will take back any puppy who they have produced and take care of him until a new home can be found, rather than see him placed in a rescue program.

Rescue groups present a great benefit to these dogs because they will see to it that they are spayed or neutered and have a complete health check by a vet. Health issues and other concerns are resolved before the adoptee is placed in his new home. If you find a Cavalier in a shelter, it is in all likelihood a lost dog with an owner seeking to find him.

THE HEALTHY PUPPY

Once you have decided where to get your Cavalier, it's important to choose a healthy dog. It doesn't matter if you obtain your canine friend from a breeder or a rescue organization; the bottom line is that he should be in the best possible health so that you can share a lifetime of happiness together.

Appearance

All puppies will seem adorable and immediately capture your heart, but knowing what to look for will alert you to any indications of potential problems that may lie ahead. The healthy Cavalier puppy comes in four colors, two genders, and many sizes. He should be plump, playful or cuddly, depending on his temperament, and have the look and feel of a hearty little dog. The eyes should be bright and without discharge in the corners. The tongue should be pink and aimed directly at your nose. The coat should be clean, shiny, and intact, with no bare spots.

Temperament

All puppies, just like all babies, have different personalities. Some puppies are quiet and watchful; some are playful and active. Some will warm up to you immediately, and some may take a bit of time to feel that they want to shower you with kisses. Try to allow the puppy some time to make up his mind about how he wishes to proceed with you. Sit quietly and allow him to approach you. Talk to him softly and let him hear the gentle tone of your voice.

Before bringing your new Cavalier home, puppy-proof your home and yard to ensure his safety.

Hold him close for a moment to allow him to feel safe. Cavalier puppies are more intuitive than many other breeds of dog. By allowing a puppy to get to know you, you will be more likely to make a good choice when it comes time to select the one you take home with you.

Many books will recommend doing various tests to check the dominance of a puppy. These tests do not apply to Cavaliers. They are the least wolf-like of all varieties of dog and will rarely attempt to be dominant toward you. Therefore, you won't learn a great deal about a Cavalier by flipping him over on his back other than that he would prefer to be upright. Rather, watch the puppy or puppies carefully as they play together. If possible, try to see them in their own environment with their mother and littermates. This is the best way to see a puppy's true temperament. If he is kept in a dog room or puppy nursery most of the time and then brought out to see prospective buyers, you may not have an opportunity to really see how he will behave once you have taken him home. Keep in mind that a puppy who has just met you may be a little overwhelmed by the experience. Try to overlook his first-time jitters and base your judgment on his overall qualities. Once you have the Cavalier puppy home, he will settle in and become a delightful companion with no memory of having pulled his littermate across the floor by the ear when you met for the first time!

PREPARING YOUR HOME AND YARD

Before bringing your puppy to his new home, you must prepare for his arrival. Puppies, being adventuresome little creatures, will sniff out everything in your home and yard that you will wish they hadn't found. They have a unique gift for being successful in "seek and destroy" missions, so you must puppy-proof any areas your puppy will have access to, both to protect your possessions and to ensure his safety.

Indoor Safety

Homes present more dangers to dogs than you may know. For the time being, keep all houseplants out of reach. Many are poisonous and will need to be removed; even when out of reach, plants can drop leaves onto the floor, which may present a danger to your pet if they are consumed. Puppies also can't resist digging in the dirt and can make quite a mess.

Puppies are particularly fond of chewing, especially on electrical cords like all those tempting ones around your desk and computer area. Most wires do not require more than a moment of serious gnawing before they can be conquered. There are several ways to protect your wiring and your dog. Either lift the wires off the floor and secure them behind furniture or enclose them in plastic tubing like the PVC piping found in hardware stores. While you may be focused on saving your computer and phone wires from the little razor-sharp teeth of an energetic puppy with boundless energy, don't forget to protect other appliance and lamp cords as well.

By the way, Cavaliers are not really very bad about chewing, but they do occasionally find something in the house to chew on—and it is usually the wrong thing! A leather couch or chair is sometimes viewed by a puppy as a giant rawhide chewy. Since you can't remove your furniture, purchase a bitter apple spray and be prepared to saturate any area of a couch, chair, or table that he may turn into a teething ring. Try to remember to keep shoes off the floor for a while as well. If you provide your puppy with good-quality chew toys like Nylabones, that too will help to prevent chewing problems. Telling a puppy "no" and removing him from the object of interest is not effective unless you replace it with an acceptable chewy or toy.

Almost anything can tempt a curious puppy. Items such as dangling tablecloths or cords from window blinds are ripe for a tug or tumble, as are decorations or anything that looks like a toy to the untrained canine eye. Also, store poisonous household cleaners and other toxic substances, as well as antifreeze, securely away from your sleuthing four-paws. Clean up spills thoroughly and dispose of containers for hazardous products where your dog can't get at them.

Dogs of all ages can die from swallowing all sorts of unlikely things, like pins, needles, string, razor blades, bottle caps, and sometimes even pieces of socks or undergarments. They can also

ingest foods or human products that may be harmful to them, such as chocolate, grapes, raisins, medicines, vitamins, and tobacco products, some of which can also kill. Teach all family members, especially your kids, to put things away; they're usually more willing when the puppy's well-being is at stake.

Outdoor Hazards

Dangers to your puppy are not only found indoors. Outdoor hazards will need to be kept in check as well. Examine your yard carefully. Remember that you can no longer use the same yard products that were fine to use before you had a dog. Get into the habit of reading labels, and eliminate any gardening supplies containing poisons that can hurt your dog. Pesticides designed to kill snails also kill several dogs a year. You can find numerous products designed specifically to be safe for pets.

Examine your roses and any other shrubs that have long thorns to see if they need to be trimmed back, fenced off, or removed to protect your dog from being injured; his eyes or body can become easily scratched.

Make sure all fencing is secure. Check for holes or other instabilities that may allow your dog a means to escape or give predators a way to enter. If you are unable to puppy-proof your whole yard, consider fencing in a smaller area just for your dog. Also, because Cavalier puppies are very appealing, a pet left

Shopping List

The following are some basic supplies your new Cavalier will need:

- crate
- bedding
- food
- bowls
- collar
- leash
- safe toys
- treats
- brush
- nail clipper

A collar needs to be properly fitted for safety and comfort. An adjustable nylon collar is a good choice for a Cavalier puppy.

unattended in the front yard is an invitation for theft. Having some sort of a locking device on your gate or installing an alarm may be a good idea. Of course, it's always best never to leave your dog unsupervised or out of sight for more than a brief period.

SUPPLIES

Just as with humans, moving into and adjusting to an unfamiliar environment can be a stressful experience for a puppy or an adult dog. When your Cavalier arrives at his new home, you should have everything ready so that he has a comfortable and safe place to settle into. If you are still in the process of preparing a permanent spot for your pet, his homecoming will be a miserable and anxious time because he will continually have to adjust to changing situations. Being able to provide for all his needs and wants upon his arrival will help make him feel secure and more likely to bond with you sooner.

Bowls and Food

Of course, food and water dishes are necessary items. Stainless steel bowls are your best choice. They last forever, they are heavy enough so that your dog can't tip them over, and they will not leach plastic by-products into the food or water. Although initially

Cavaliers love toys and, unlike some breeds of dog, they often keep them for years.

more expensive, they are the only bowls you will ever have to buy.

While you are shopping, pick up a bag of the food that the puppy has been eating. Even though your breeder probably gave you a starter supply, you will need to buy food within a few days. As discussed, it's not a good idea to change the puppy's diet abruptly. His digestive system is delicate and not yet used to a variety of foods. He started with breast milk and then was slowly switched over to the food that he was eating at the time of purchase. Puppies should also not be given dog treats and chews.

Collar and Leash

A collar needs to be properly fitted for safety and comfort. Therefore, wait until you can take your puppy into the pet store with you before you buy his collar. All pet stores welcome well-behaved dogs, and all dogs love to go on trips with their parents. View the short trip for a beginner's collar as an important first outing for your puppy. However, do not take him out of your home until after he has had his second immunization, when it will be safe for him to be exposed to other dogs and unfamiliar environments.

Never purchase choke chains or chains designed for training a recalcitrant dog. Your Cavalier puppy should need no more than a soft nylon collar that is well-fitted to avoid pinching or leaving enough space for him to slip his head through and escape. Once you have enrolled your puppy or adult dog in obedience classes, the instructor may have a different suggestion as to a collar that would be more appropriate for training purposes.

You will also need to purchase a light- to medium-weight leash. Leather leashes last a very long time and are less likely to show dirt or staining. They are more expensive initially as well, but in the long run will end up saving you the purchase price of several of the lighter colored fabric leads.

Crate

Crating your dog may appear to be a cruel practice, but it is actually a kindness. Dogs are denning animals, and they appreciate the privacy and comfort of a little den that they can call their own. A crate is also the best tool for keeping your puppy and belongings safe. It is useful when housetraining or traveling, and it offers a place where your dog can feel secure if he is injured or ill. It provides a safe haven when you're not home, and it will help prevent unwanted behaviors by keeping your dog confined when you can't watch him. Any time you are not able to supervise your puppy, place him into his crate and give him a chew toy or favorite stuffed animal. Although he may complain at first, he will quickly learn to love it. When you transport your puppy or adult dog, he will need to be confined in a crate (such as the ones Nylabone makes) for his protection.

Dog crates come in wire, plastic, and aluminum, on wheels, with handles, and in various colors and sizes. An adult Cavalier needs a medium-sized crate approximately 24 inches (61 cm) high by 18 inches (46 cm) wide. If you purchase the medium-sized kennel from the start, you will not have to make another purchase later. Be sure the door fits well and latches securely so that paws and teeth can't open it. Most people like to provide bedding in the crate, but if your pup likes to rip things to shreds, forego the bedding until he outgrows his urge to shred. If you decide to purchase a pad, it should be soft and comfortable for cuddling but very washable.

Toys

Cavaliers love toys, and unlike some breeds of dog, they often keep them for years. Many prefer human baby toys over dog toys. They especially love small stuffed animals that can be firmly grasped in their teeth and carried about. Some will often form an attachment to a specific toy and enjoy sleeping with it every

night of their lives. For safety reasons, avoid purchasing stuffed toys that have beans or other small objects in them and stick with soft polyester-filled toys without buttons or other removal objects. "Stuffies" will give your Cavalier hours of play and pleasure. Remember that they too should be thrown into the washing machine along with crate pads and given a good washing from time to time. The best place to find stuffed toys is at thrift stores. They are less expensive there than at any other place and the variety can't be beat.

Other toys that puppies will enjoy are balls (of the correct size for his age), tug toys, and chewable objects. From the time they cut their teeth until the time that they are losing them, chew toys are a favorite of every dog. When your puppy or dog has chewed a toy down to an inch of its original size or has broken it, discreetly take it from him and dispose of it. Toys in this condition are no longer safe and can cause a choking hazard or bowel obstruction. Always make sure that any toys you give your dog are safe and nontoxic.

Grooming Supplies

Most pet stores and large discount retail stores are a great place to purchase the grooming supplies that you will need. You can stock up on shampoo, conditioner, combs, brushes, and a nail trimmer. Read over the section of this book about grooming your Cavalier before making your choices.

Some larger pet stores have grooming facilities and can often bathe and dry your dog while you do your shopping, although appointments are usually required. Your dog may look forward to these outings, and they can provide wonderful bonding time for both of you.

Identification

Proper identification can save your dog's life, and it can also help him get returned to you if he ever gets lost. Every dog should wear an identification tag with your phone number on it. You can also consider a permanent form of ID as well. Your veterinarian can insert a microchip—a transmitter about the size of a grain of rice—under the skin between your dog's shoulders, or you can have your dog tattooed with an identifying number, normally on the belly or flanks. For more information, check with your veterinarian.

TRAVELING WITH YOUR DOG

If you choose to travel with your dog, you'll need to make some basic preparations for his travel needs and safety. Of course, when traveling by car, your Cavalier will need to be confined in a well-secured kennel or crate while the car is in motion. You can give him a toy and a few chews to keep him occupied. If possible, position the crate so that your Cavalier can see outside the car, which can also help him to pass the time during the trip.

A leash is needed for safely walking your dog at rest areas along the way and for his visit at your destination. Some locales require that all dogs be leashed regardless of their size. A portable little water dish will be useful, particularly one that can be attached to the inside door of the kennel. When traveling longer than a day, you'll need to bring along food, bowls, and some toys to make your dog feel secure in unfamiliar surroundings.

Be sure to stop at least every 4 to 5 hours to allow your Cavalier time to potty and stretch his legs. During every rest stop, walk him briskly for a few minutes—this will be good for him as well as for the driver and passengers.

Airline Travel

If you are flying with your Cavalier, you can purchase a lightweight, soft carrier. These travel bags are designed to be safe, very portable, and comfortable for small dogs. They have mesh siding that lets air easily pass in and out, as well as offering visibility from inside the carrier. They also are designed to fit under airplane seats, and they can be carried on board if you make prior arrangements with the airlines. However, there is always a fee for this, and reservations are a must. Although you are not allowed to take your dog out of the carrier, once on board he can sit on your lap inside the carrier. Soft-sided little dog carriers such as these come in a wheeled version with a handle too. Think of the possibilities!

If you are planning to travel with your Cavalier using one of these soft carriers, practice with him well before the trip. Allow him to become familiar with it. Let him nap in it for several days. You can even place your puppy in the carrier for short car trips around town while running errands. By giving him time to become accustomed to being in it, he will not be overly excited or agitated when the real travel day arrives.

Travel Etiquette

During your travels, and certainly when you arrive at your destination, practice good manners. Unfortunately, some pet owners have behaved in ways that have made dogs unwelcome in many public places, either by letting their pets run loose or by not cleaning up after them. Be courteous if you are a guest in someone's home or if you are staying in a hotel room with your Cavalier. Don't leave him alone to bark or cause problems, and bring a sheet to spread over beds or chairs where your dog may rest.

Going Cargo

The other option for air travel with your Cavalier is to fly him in the cargo hold of the plane. This is less desirable because you have less control over how your dog is managed by the airline staff, but it may be the only option for larger dogs who don't fit into small, soft-sided carrier bags.

To fly your dog cargo, you must make a reservation with the cargo department of the airline. Some will only carry a limited number of dogs on any one connection, so reserve early. Plan to pay a fee that is determined by the destination and duration of the flight. The fee for shipping a dog or puppy in this manner varies, and like all other goods and services, goes up every year.

An airline-approved kennel or crate (soft-sided or collapsible crates are never allowed in cargo) and proper documentation will be required. Two small food and water dishes must be attached to the inside of the crate. You can fill one dish with water the night before and freeze it. This will prevent water from splashing around in the crate during handling and transport. Lots of dogs love ice and will view this as a big treat.

Other Considerations

When flying, a few more considerations may help your dog travel more comfortably. For example, it may be necessary to reconfigure his feeding schedule; it's best not to feed him the morning of the flight; instead, give him an extra helping at dinner the night before. It's also a good idea to fill a small bag with kibble and attach it securely to the kennel in case the plane is grounded and the dog requires feeding. In all likelihood it won't be needed, but it is a good precaution to take.

Also allow your dog to have a good run in the morning because he will be confined a great portion of the day. Take him for one more walk in the cargo department before placing him into the kennel or crate. Do the same upon arrival.

Be sure that you have attached "live animal" stickers to the crate, and place the name of your pet, as well as your name and contact information, on the kennel for the baggage handlers' information. Any time you ship your dog in cargo, ensure him for his full value. Sadly, some dogs do get lost in transit.

Travel Documents

Before taking your puppy or adult dog on an airplane, you must get a health certificate from your vet 10 days prior to traveling. The health certificate must either state that your dog is too young to have received the rabies vaccine or the dates on which he was immunized, the type of vaccine used, and the serial number. If you are going to be gone longer than 10 days, the airline may require a new health certificate prior to boarding the plane for your return trip. Call the airline well ahead of time and inquire as to their specific rules, regulations, and fees regarding travel with pets.

Traveling with your Cavalier can be a tremendous amount of fun, whether you travel by car or by plane. Besides, your dog would always rather be with you whenever possible.

When You Can't Take Your Cavalier

Occasionally, you may have to travel and find yourself unable to take your new puppy or dog along. What do you do?

Many breeders will board dogs they have placed. There may or may not be a small fee for room and board, but you can rest assured that your Cavalier will be left in good hands. You'll need to make an appointment in advance because most breeders are unable to care for more than one or two dogs besides their own at a time. Sometimes, you can negotiate a boarding agreement into your puppy contract at the time of purchase.

Finding a Pet Sitter

The National Association of Professional Pet Sitters (NAPPS) is a nonprofit group that certifies and screens experienced pet sitters for knowledge and integrity. To find a member near you, visit www.petsitters.org or call them toll-free at 1-800-296-PETS.

A good pet sitter should:

- have commercial liability coverage insurance (and provide proof)
- be bonded (so you are protected against theft)
- keep written records of your dog's special needs, habits, diet, routine, and medicine
- be able and willing to transport your dog to your vet or an emergency clinic if the need arises
- have a backup for herself in case of an emergency on her end (and be able to provide you with that information upon request)
- provide a written contract that clearly specifies her responsibilities, including medicating or grooming your dog
- provide references and contact information

Boarding Kennels

If your breeder is unable to take your dog, boarding kennels are always an option. These facilities do a good job of keeping your pet safe, but the care he receives is usually minimal. Boarded dogs are often kept in a run of some sort, with a door leading to the outdoors for pottying. This is bare-bones dog care, but your Cavalier will most likely be well fed and protected in your absence. Ask for referrals from your vet or from friends and neighbors who have pets. Visit several kennels before choosing one, and ask lots of questions. Of course, make sure that the facilities are clean and that the boarders look well attended. Most kennels will require that all immunizations are current.

Pet Sitters

If at all possible, the best alternative for your dog's care when you are away from home is to leave him with a professional dog sitter. Again, ask your vet, friends, and neighbors for referrals. Local pet stores may offer suggestions, and in this age of the Internet, it may be fairly easy to find one online. Simply type in "dog sitter" and your geographical area and a list of animal-loving people will appear.

Needless to say, when trusting someone to come to your home and care for your pet, it is always a good idea to interview prospective candidates thoroughly. Always ask for qualifications, references, and whether the person or organization is insured. Ask questions such as: How often will the dog sitter visit, and how long will she stay? Will she need to bring anyone else into your home? Can she drive your dog to the vet in case of an emergency? Make a list of the things that you need to know in order to feel comfortable with this person taking care of your dog in your home.

The best advantage to enlisting the services of a dog sitter is that your Cavalier will not have to leave home and can remain in a comfortable environment while you are gone. Your dog can also have some much-needed company. If you're lucky, dog sitters can also be house sitters; they can bring in the mail, turn lights on and off, water your houseplants, and in general, keep an eye on things.

Doggy Day Care

These days, working dog parents have the lovely option of bringing their canine kids to doggy day care. Numerous small facilities cater to the various needs of owners who work far from home. Special attention is paid to the temperament of the dogs who are cared for in these facilities; doggy guests are often allowed to socialize with each other, so good behavior and good manners are a must. These facilities require all immunizations as well. This is also another option for care if you are only going to be away from home for a day.

FEEDING

Your Cavalier King Charles Spaniel

There are almost as many feeding schedules, feeding preparations, and preferences available to you as there are dogs on the planet. Diets range from those that are completely raw and natural, to those that are home-cooked and organic, and even to bags of kibble stored in the barn.

So you can well imagine that the topic of feeding canines is an interesting one to all breeders, as well as to owners who want to give their dogs the best possible nutrition. Every imaginable type of feeding protocol is debated and discussed with vigor. Tempers can flare and friendships can teeter when people engage in the hot topic of what constitutes appropriate foods for their beloved canine companions. Proponents of raw diets would never dream of feeding kibble, and dyed-in-the-wool kibble feeders often react to the raw diet as if you announced you were feeding your dog a diet of dead mice and small bugs. There seems to be no middle ground in this lively debate. The truth of the matter is that the there are valid points about every option among this vast array of choices.

Dogs are opportunistic feeders in their natural state, and no wild dog worth his salt would ever turn down a bowl of raw organic food any more than he would refuse a bowl of kibble straight out of the barn. For that matter, any self-respecting wild dog would also gobble up the previously mentioned fictional diet of dead mice and small bugs while he was at it. Dogs are reasonably flexible and willing to eat just about anything we provide as long as we provide in it ample quantities and on time. By looking at their teeth we would guess that dogs are carnivores—animals who eat meat. But by looking at their feeding habits, we see that they are also opportunistic omnivores—animals that eat both plants and animals. Cavaliers are the same. They will enjoy a piece of raw meat, but they will certainly have no objection to sharing your bag of potato chips or licking your ice cream dish clean—although those aren't very healthy choices for him.

FOOD BASICS

Living organisms of all types require food in order to maintain their bodies. Foods are made of several different components: carbohydrates, fats, proteins, vitamins, minerals, and water. These ingredients comprise the building blocks of nutrition. A discussion of the various components, or building blocks, of food will help you to understand your dog's need for a nutritionally balanced diet.

Carbohydrates

There is an ongoing debate among animal nutritionists regarding carbohydrates in the diet of dogs. Dogs are able to convert proteins and carbohydrates into both muscle tissue and energy, and the debate mainly focuses on how much carbohydrate should be included in the commercially prepared dog foods available to us.

In the wild, wolves and wild dogs are not known to consume large amounts of carbohydrates, so based on this reasoning one would infer that domestic dogs do not require them in quantity either. And yet we know that they are drawn to them and will eat them in large quantities if given the opportunity. Commercially prepared dog foods are designed to contain rather large amounts of carbohydrates such as rice, wheat, and corn. The main issue with feeding excessive amounts of these carbohydrates is that they can cause obesity and digestive issues.

If your dog is overweight or has a lot of gas, bloating, or diarrhea, look first at the carbohydrate content of the foods you are feeding, and consider switching to a diet that is higher in protein and lower in carbohydrates to offset these effects. Most dog food labels are clear about the contents of the food, but when in doubt, discuss food choices with your vet. When you think carbs, think primarily of energy value.

Fats

Small amounts of fat in the diet are absolutely necessary, even for an overweight dog. A healthy dog's body will contain fat stores that are not an indication of obesity. These fat stores are necessary for good health because they supply a source of energy at times when food supplies are low, and they act as a storage depot for various fat-soluble vitamins and minerals. Fat stores in reasonable amounts also help a dog's body to stay warm in times of cold weather.

Your Cavalier's daily diet should contain the proper amount of proteins, vitamins, minerals, and other essential nutrients.

A general rule of thumb to use when determining the correct amount of dietary fat for your dog is to look for foods that provide around 28 percent protein for puppies and 18 percent for adult pets who enjoy a normal activity level.

The best indication of whether or not your dog is getting enough fats in his daily diet is to determine if he is at the correct weight for his body frame. If he is underweight, increase his food ration. If he is overweight, consider putting him on a proper diet. An easy way to do this is to cut his food ration by one-third and to replace the volume of that one-third with plain canned pumpkin. Dogs like the taste of pumpkin, and it is low in calories and high in fiber so they feel full but can still slowly lose the excess weight. Discuss safe dieting options with your vet beforehand. You can also ask about the advisability of giving your dog a canine multivitamin while he is on a lower calorie diet.

Minerals

Four primary minerals must be present in your dog's diet. These are calcium, magnesium, phosphorus, and sulfur. The most important of these are calcium and phosphorus, especially for growing puppies. Calcium is generally thought to play a role in the formation of strong bones and teeth, but it actually plays a more important role in muscle contractibility, which includes the heart muscle. It assists the blood to clot, and it activates a variety of enzymes that affect cellular activity and health. Phosphorus, too, affects almost all the chemical reactions within your pet's body. Read the labels on dog foods you buy, and make sure that minerals are listed in the contents.

Proteins

Proteins are important in every aspect of your dog's growth and development. They are essential building blocks for both structural makeup and for the immune system. But protein is not stored in the body, so your Cavalier must obtain a fresh supply from his food every day.

To be sure your dog consumes enough protein, check the protein values of the foods he consumes. These values are measured using eggs as a measuring stick; an egg has a protein value of 100, which is a high level. Fish meal and milk are next, with a protein value of 92. For the most part, the highest protein values come from animal sources. Meats, eggs, and dairy are major sources, but soy beans do offer a protein value of 67. Judge the quality of the proteins in your dog food by the products that are listed on the label; contents provided in the greatest quantities are listed first. The best choices will show chicken and lamb as the first ingredients. Chicken and meat by-products are not as digestible as meat and should be considered of lower nutritional value.

Calorie Guide

The calorie content per cup will vary somewhat among the different brands of kibble or types of food you feed your dog. The best way to determine the correct amount to feed is to read food labels and use the calorie counts provided.

To stay healthy, active, and trim, a 10-pound Cavalier needs 400 to 500 calories per day, a 15-pound Cavalier needs 600 to 700 calories a day, and a 20-pound Cavalier needs 700 to 800 calories per day. Divide food into two or three small daily meals. If your dog still appears to be hungry but his weight is appropriate for his size, supplement his meals with low-calorie, fat-free foods like canned pumpkin. Don't guess on quantities; use a measuring cup.

Water is critical to your Cavalier's good health. Always make fresh, clean water available to him daily, indoors and out.

Vitamins

No discussion about optimal nutrition would be complete without a brief discussion about vitamins. Vitamins are divided into two basic groups: water soluble and fat soluble.

Water-soluble vitamins are more or less dissolved in water and then dispersed throughout the body to do their jobs. These include B vitamins (thiamin, riboflavin, niacin, pantothenic acid, pyridoxine, cyanocobalamin, folic acid, and biotin) and vitamin C.

Other vitamins are fat soluble, which means that they can only be dissolved if the food that is fed has a certain amount of fat in it. Fat-soluble vitamins are vitamin A, D, E, and K.

The primary difference between the two groups is that fat-soluble vitamins are stored in the liver and fatty tissues of the body, while water-soluble vitamins are present in the body in only very small amounts. Fat-soluble vitamins need to be taken in daily, either through diet or supplementation, because any excess is excreted by the body.

If you are feeding a high-quality, healthy food, particularly one that is fortified with additional vitamins and minerals, and if your dog appears to be healthy and energetic with a good-quality coat and no apparent problems, you probably do not need to provide a daily vitamin supplementation to puppies or adults. However, older dogs absorb fewer vitamins and minerals through the intestinal tract because of their advanced age and may well benefit from the daily addition of a good-quality supplement.

Discuss giving your dog vitamins and other supplements with your vet beforehand, and take his advice regarding this important topic. If your dog is extremely active or involved in dog sports such as agility, you may want to consider giving him vitamin supplements. As already mentioned, if you are putting your Cavalier on a weight-loss program, you may also want to consider supplementation to offset the loss of vitamins resulting from eating smaller quantities of food.

As with all other areas of nutrition, there is some controversy about vitamin supplementation. Some breeders, along with some vets, believe that it is absolutely essential for all dogs. Because commercial dog foods are cooked, steamed, and processed, they feel that essential vitamins may be lacking. Do your own research, read the labels on your dog food choices, and discuss proper nutrition with your vet in order to make a confident decision. One thing is certain: If you decide to supplement your dogs' diet with vitamins, use just one product to prevent oversupplementation, which can harm your dog.

Water

Water is an essential component of your dog's optimal health. It aids in digestion and in the maintenance of normal body temperature, and it is used to convert nutritional fuel into energy.

A dog's body is made up of 70 percent water. However, if a dog loses even 10 percent of his normal water stores, he will become severely dehydrated and can die. Throughout the day, small particles of water are exhaled along with his breath. He also loses water when he urinates. As he metabolizes both food and water, his body is using and losing water stores, so they must be replenished constantly.

To prevent problems, make sure your dog has a bowl of fresh, clean water available to him at all times. Keeping one bowl inside the house and another one outside in the yard is always a good idea. Putting bowls close to a water source helps make cleaning and refilling them easier.

FEEDING FACTORS TO CONSIDER

When it comes to deciding what you are going to feed your dog, there are many factors to consider, including your personal biases toward food, your dog's specific dietary needs and restrictions (if any), cost, and the time necessary to prepare specialized diets. Even kitchen storage and counter space available for preparation should be considered before you commit to any specific regimen.

Dietary Requirements and Age

Your dog's nutritional requirements are determined by age; puppies will have different needs than adults or seniors, as will pregnant females. For example, puppy foods are nutritionally geared toward growth patterns. Some breeders only feed puppy food while the dog is very young. Once he gets to be three or four months old, they will switch him to adult food to avoid a rapid growth pattern that might lead to bone and joint problems later in life. Other breeders have had good luck sticking with a good-quality puppy food until the puppy is a year old or even older. Talk to your breeder about why she has chosen the particular food she feeds.

Adult dogs in their prime can eat just about any dog food and thrive. Some foods seem to put more coat on dogs. Some are better for their teeth. And some will produce fewer waste products and subsequently less stool. Commercial foods are designed to offer balanced nutrition and address a variety of special needs. But your dog has to like it in order to be happy eating it.

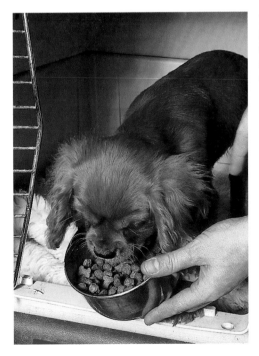

Your dog's nutritional requirements are determined by age; puppies will have different needs than adults or seniors.

Your Dog's Preferences

Although canines are opportunistic in their eating habits (basically, they will eat just about anything they have an opportunity to eat), they do have individual preferences much in the same way that their human owners do. Some like canned food, others prefer dry kibble. Some like beef flavor, others prefer chicken. Some like vegetables and fruits, and some are content with just about anything you are willing to put into their bowls. As long as you take your time in changing from one food to another and introduce new items gradually, you are free to try any nutritionally complete combination that you think might work well for both you and your Cavalier.

CHOOSING THE RIGHT FOOD

Start your search for dog food by choosing the category your dog most closely fits. Is he a puppy or an adult? Is he a senior? Is he underweight or overweight? Has he ever experienced allergic reactions to specific foods in the past? Does he lead an active lifestyle with lots of physical activity, or is he primarily in the house leading a quiet, sedate life? Once you have determined which issues your Cavalier deals with, you are ready to start learning about the foods he will require.

Commercial Diets

Luckily for those of us on a busy schedule, several different types of commercially prepared dog foods are available. At almost any large grocery store, you can find dry kibble, semi-moist foods packaged in convenient little tear-top bags, and canned foods. You can also buy frozen dog foods that generally contain more meats and thus higher protein content.

While many dog owners and breeders have strong opinions about the kind of food that they prefer to feed their dogs, it appears that dogs often thrive on any nutritionally complete food. A discussion about the different kinds of foods available, as well as a recognition of the calories that your particular dog may need, will be helpful to you as you shop for prepared diets for your pet.

Dry Food (Kibble)

Dogs find kibble to be a perfectly acceptable food, including Cavaliers. Dry foods come in almost every price range. Large

Reading Dog Food Labels

Regardless of what kind of commercial dog food you choose, look for a statement on the packaging saying that the food meets the American Association of Feed Control Officials (AAFCO) guidelines. The AAFCO is the governing body for all animal feed products, and its guidelines ensure that the food was prepared safely and that it meets specific nutritional levels. But it's still up to you to choose the food that best meets your own dog's needs based on his age, weight, and reproductive status.

An animal-based protein should be one of the first five ingredients listed. Ideally, it should be one of the first three. Beef, chicken, turkey, and lamb are the usual types of meat contained in commercial foods. Don't be put off by "meat by-products." You might not want to eat them, but they are good for your dog. By-products include organ meats, and they can be a rich source of protein, vitamins, and minerals. The food should not contain hooves, horns, feathers, fur, or manure.

Check the label for added sugars. It may say sugar, or it may say corn syrup or sucrose. These sugars are unnecessary and add empty calories to your dog's food, so try to avoid them. Preservatives, if any, also will be listed on the label. If you prefer a dog food with natural preservatives, buy smaller quantities to ensure freshness.

discount stores often sell good-quality kibble in very large bags, which are a good value for the money. Grocery stores sell bagged kibble in a variety of sizes, too. Specialized pet stores will frequently have a variety of dry kibbles available, including their own store brands, which are acceptable in all ways to your dog.

Many breeders feed nothing but kibble and occasional healthy treats to their dogs for the length of their lives. Kibble's main advantage to you is that it is relatively inexpensive, it can be purchased in bulk, and it can be kept for long periods of time when properly stored. Read labels carefully before purchase, however, to make sure that the food provides a well-balanced diet.

Canned (Wet) Food

Canned dog foods smell and taste great to your dog, but their soft consistency is thought to create a buildup of plaque and tartar on teeth, so they should be used sparingly. They can be offered as a small portion of the regular diet or added to kibble to increase flavor, but generally should be avoided as the only food being fed. Read labels to find a brand that offers the most nutrition.

Semi-Moist Food

Semi-moist foods tend to come in small, individually sized packages. Some are even shaped like burgers or other meaty-looking tidbits. They are generally the most expensive option in the pet aisle, but they often don't offer adequate nutrition all on their own. These, too, are considered by many breeders to add to the problem of plaque and tartar buildup on the teeth and should be used sparingly and not fed long-term.

They are great for travel, though, because they are convenient, clean, do not require refrigeration, and are easy to feed to your dog. Many Cavaliers have digestive difficulties if switched from one food to another, so before considering using semi-moist foods while away from home, give your dog a trial run at home and watch for diarrhea or increased gas.

Noncommercial Diets

Many dog owners prefer to feed a diet that they have prepared themselves. Sometimes these diets consist of raw meaty bones combined with raw veggies that have been blended to assist in digestion. Other times, these home-prepared, noncommercial diets are cooked, divided into small portions, frozen, and fed daily. Learning about the pros and cons of these diets will help you to come to your own decision about feeding them to your Cavalier.

The Home-Cooked Diet

Preparing a dog's meals at home allows an owner to know exactly what her pet is eating, and also lets her add her own particular brand of TLC.

One popular recipe for a home-cooked diet is to combine a few pounds of ground meat (beef, chicken, or turkey), some fresh or frozen vegetables (green beans, peas, carrots, squash, etc.), and a couple of cups of rice in a pot of water, and then boil the mixture until everything is cooked. Once cooled, you can package the mixture into smaller quantities and store them in your freezer. Another popular diet is to boil chicken breasts and add both the juices and cut up chicken to the regular diet of kibble. Dogs love this but will often learn to pick through the meal to take out just the chicken and leave the kibble.

In my experience, dogs quickly grow tired of each new recipe. Another crucial drawback is that it's difficult to get the balance of

A carefully designed home-cooked diet can have many advantages for dogs with special needs. Check with your vet to make sure that this type of diet is right for your Cavalier.

vitamins and minerals correct. If you choose to prepare a home-cooked diet for your Cavalier, do some careful research so that you can learn how to balance it with the addition of the necessary vitamins, minerals, and other supplements. Discuss this option with your vet before switching your dog's diet.

There are circumstances in which a dog may benefit greatly from eating a home-cooked diet. Specialty diets are a good alternative for dogs who suffer from a variety of diseases. Cavaliers afflicted with heart disease, kidney or urinary tract diseases, obesity, or diabetes, as well food allergies, can certainly benefit from being given foods that deal with these problems, which can help them maintain better health.

The Raw Food Diet

Many breeders and pet owners prefer not to feed commercially prepared dog foods and instead choose to feed a raw diet because they believe it is a more natural way for dogs to eat.

Raw diets are based on what a wolf in the wild might consume. Wolves, from whom domestic dogs are descended, eat a raw diet composed of whatever they are able to either kill or find within their territories. Being meat eaters, both wolves and dogs have teeth that are designed specifically for doing so: enlarged, elongated, and sharp teeth tear meat into edible portions, canines hold onto prey, and molars crush bones. Not only do they not chew their food, but their mouth is designed for swallowing large portions quickly; saliva plays no part in the digestion of food.

The digestive tracts of carnivores and omnivores are short, simple, and far better suited to digesting meat, fat, and bones than plants. To compare, look at the more complex digestive tract of a domesticated cow. It includes four separate stomachs so that a cow is able to regurgitate hay or other plant materials for further chewing after it has already been swallowed and partially digested. Cows have large molar teeth for chewing this regurgitated cud and spend hours "processing" their food. Dogs, on the other hand, have a short digestive tract, one stomach, strong stomach acids, and teeth that were never intended for chewing. Proponents of raw diets look to these basic differences between meat eaters and plant eaters as proof that a diet containing corn, wheat, barley, and rice is not beneficial or suitable for a dog.

Raw Foods for Your Cavalier

Proponents of raw diets, sometimes known as bones and raw food (BARF) diets, believe that 60 percent of your dog's diet should consist of raw meaty bones and 40 percent should consist of "a wide variety of human food scraps," mostly raw vegetables and fruits.

The bulk of the raw diet usually consists of raw chicken and turkey bones, with organ meat (liver, kidney, heart, brain, tongue, and tripe) and eggs added periodically. Green leafy vegetables are also included in the diet and are usually run through a food processor or juicer. Vegetable oil, brewers yeast, kelp, apple cider vinegar, fresh and dried fruits, and raw honey are often added. Some people give their dogs small portions of grain products, and some add dairy products, especially raw goat's milk, cottage cheese, and plain yogurt. This diet is not recommended for gestational bitches because of the high level of calcium.

Safety

The main issue that comes up in discussions about raw diets is their safety. The main concern is fear of contamination by bacteria and parasites such as salmonella. This is based on the widely held belief of pet owners, breeders, and vets alike that humans have the potential to contract them from handling raw meats. Pet food manufacturers, unsurprisingly, mention salmonella frequently in the written materials that advertise their own foods. Little mention, however, is made of the fact that there have been many recalls of dry dog foods due to pathogens found growing in them. Recently, over 70 dogs died from a mold they ingested while eating a popular brand of dry kibble.

All foods have the potential to carry microscopic organisms of one type or another. If not salmonella, then it could be another bacteria or one of the many varieties of molds and toxins that adversely affect humans and dogs alike. But it's not the foods that you feed— these organisms are everywhere—but how they are handled, what kinds of cleaning techniques are utilized, and how they are stored that is going to make a difference. Nothing is perfectly safe, and in the same way that we expect to accept responsibility for what we consume, so must we be willing to accept responsibility for the safety of the foods that our dogs consume.

Use care when preparing raw foods. Clean cutting boards and countertops with a 10 percent bleach solution whether you are preparing meat or chicken for your family or your dog. Wash your hands after handling raw meats and before handling other foods. Clean all raw vegetables separately. The vast majority of salmonellosis in humans is acquired by eating human foods purchased at supermarket or in restaurants, not from handling the raw foods that you feed to your dogs.

Dogs also do a lot of "licky-sniffy" activities, most of them in fairly unappealing spots such as toilet bowels, garbage cans, animal feces, and private areas on other canines. These habits have a far greater tendency to contaminate and infect their human caregivers than does eating properly handled raw foods.

So, does this mean that commercially prepared foods are safer than raw foods? Not necessarily. All foods have the potential for health risk to some degree. Proper handling and storage of food is of utmost importance in protecting your dog. Speedy and appropriate disposal of dog feces, no matter which diet you feed, will also help eliminate safety and health concerns.

As with any new diet, do your research, consult your vet, and introduce the raw diet to your Cavalier in stages, gradually

Meat and Plant Eaters

So, is your Cavalier a carnivore (meat eater) or an herbivore (plant eater)? Neither. Your Cavalier is an *opportunistic carnivore*, which means he can and will eat almost anything that presents itself as a food source. Keep this fact in mind as you choose among the various foods and diet options available to your dog. Overall, a well-balanced and nutritionally complete diet is what your dog requires.

decreasing the proportion of the old food and increasing that of the raw food.

Treats

From puppyhood on through their senior years, dogs love to chew—they love to chew shoes, furniture, their owner's personal belongings—well, just about everything. But they also love to chew on food treats. The right kinds of treats are great in moderation and good for the souls of dogs and owners alike, but it's very important to select healthy and safe edibles. Not all treats are created equal. It is possible to give your dog a healthful treat that he finds yummy, but choose treats as carefully as you would a dog food. Look for small treats or treats you can break into smaller pieces—you should give morsels, not mouthfuls. Avoid treats that contain sugars, food dyes, and if possible, chemical preservatives.

Dog cookies are widely available in different price ranges. They contain many of the same ingredients that are found in kibble and other dry dog foods. Sometimes they come in interesting flavors such as peanut butter or cheese. Dogs certainly enjoy them, but they should only be dispensed as a once-a-day treat.

Other healthy food treats can be found in your grocery store's produce section. Fresh carrot sticks and slices of fresh apple make excellent dog treats. Green beans are good too, and they are low in calories. They can be given frozen right out of the freezer or fresh. Cavaliers love all kinds of berries and most melons and fruits, such as peaches and apricots.

Besides food treats, artificial bones made of strong, hard material, like Nylabones, make good chew toys. Some are coated with a tasty meat or peanut butter flavor; others have a nubby texture designed to massage the dog's gums as he chews, or mint flavor to freshen his breath. These "bones" are very durable and convenient to find.

INTRODUCING A NEW FOOD

Assess how your dog looks, acts, and appears to feel after being fed a specific food for a while. If you are not satisfied, experiment and try offering some new foods. Again, it is very important to introduce new food sources gradually. If your pet is allowed to consume too much of the new food too soon, he can experience vomiting or other digestive upsets such as excess gas, constipation,

Introduce new food or treats slowly over a period of ten days or so to prevent digestive upset.

or diarrhea. This is because your dog's intestine contains normal, naturally occurring bacteria that are there to help your pet digest food, and any sudden change in diet can cause a change in the number of bacteria present, which results in upsets. Remember that when you feed your dog, you are also feeding these very necessary bacteria.

Introduce new food slowly over a period of 10 days or so. You can do this in one of two ways, depending on your preference. You can add 10 percent of the new food to his old food each day, until you have changed to the new food 100 percent. The other method involves introducing 25 percent of the new food in increments over a 10-day period. On the first day you would feed 75 percent of the old food and 25 percent of the new. On the second and third day you would repeat that formula. On the fourth day you would feed 50 percent of the old food and 50 percent of the new food, and then repeat that again on the fifth and sixth day. By the seventh day, you would be feeding 75 percent of the new food and only 25 percent of the old food. Feed that formula on day eight and nine, and by day 10 your dog's intestinal system will be ready to eat 100 percent of the new food.

While you are in the process of switching foods, watch your dog's bowel habits carefully. At the first sign of diarrhea or vomiting, back off the new food and introduce less at a time.

The same process should occur if you introduce any new treats to your Cavalier. Try them out one or two bites at a time, and watch the bowel habits of your pet carefully to make sure you have not introduced fresh fruit or veggies into his diet too quickly.

FEEDING SCHEDULES

There are basically two ways you can feed your Cavalier. You can choose to feed him on a well-maintained schedule, or you can leave a bowl of food out at all times and allow him to free feed.

Scheduled Feeding

Adult dogs need to be fed twice a day: first thing in the morning and again in the late afternoon or before your own dinner time. This will allow your dog to digest his food and have a bowel movement prior to bedtime.

Free Feeding

Cavaliers can be such little "foodaholics" that free feeding is not a good idea unless you have to deal with an emergency situation or you know in advance that you can't make it home in time for a scheduled feeding. They will eat all of their food in a short period of time and may then experience diarrhea from overfeeding.

Free feeding also deprives you of an important way to monitor your Cavalier's health. A dog's appetite and eating habits are indicators of his well-being. One of the first signs you may have that your dog isn't feeling well is a lack of appetite—a decreased interest in food at regular mealtimes may indicate a health issue. If your dog has food available all day long, you won't be able

Free Feeding Caution

Dogs are opportunistic eaters. Being very food motivated, they'll hardly ever pass up a chance to nibble on whatever tasty morsel they find. However, a dog's digestive system is not designed to accommodate continuous eating. Canines in the wild have long interludes between meals, giving their bodies a chance to digest and prepare for their next feeding. So when deciding on a feeding schedule for your Cavalier, offer a finite amount of food at designated times during the day, usually once in the morning and once in the evening. This way you'll know that your dog is getting the proper amount of food he needs to stay healthy. Opt for free feeding only when you know in advance that you can't make it home in time for a scheduled feeding.

to differentiate an atypical loss of appetite from a temporary disinterest in food.

A dog's digestive system is not designed to accommodate continuous eating. Dogs in the wild have long interludes between meals, giving their bodies a chance to digest and prepare for the next feeding. The key to a healthy, happy dog is to allow his body to function as nature intended. For your Cavalier's overall health, it's best to stick to scheduled feedings.

FEEDING FOR EVERY LIFE STAGE

Dogs are much like humans in that their feeding needs vary as they grow from babyhood into adulthood and old age. Your dog will require different foods and feeding schedules as he ages. Part of being a responsible owner is understanding your dog's changing nutritional needs at different stages of his life.

Feeding Your Cavalier Puppy

Cavalier puppies generally love foods of all kinds, and they are more than willing to eat whenever someone offers them anything. However, for the sake of his overall health and development, don't let your puppy's willingness to do this determine how and when you feed him.

Puppies require more protein and fat than adult dogs and should be given foods made specifically for their life stage. Because they are only able to eat small meals, they must also be fed more often than adults. Generally, they should be given food four times a day until they are approximately 6 months old, then three times a day for a few months, and by one year of age they should be eating two meals a day consisting of adult food.

Several good-quality puppy kibbles are on the market. The protein content in puppy kibble should be approximately 28 percent, and the fat content should be approximately 19 percent. This will allow for both fast growth and the extra fuel needed for a puppy's high energy output.

The best way to determine how much food to give your puppy per meal is to place a small amount in his bowl and see how much of it he consumes in 15 minutes. This will give you an indication of what he requires at his current growth stage. A careful examination of your puppy's body will also help you to determine if he is overweight or underweight. If you can see the puppy's ribs as he is in motion, he is probably too thin. It is normal for puppies, like human babies, to have a small amount of body fat as they are in growing stages. When in doubt, consult with your vet.

Feeding Your Cavalier Adult

As discussed, adult dogs should be fed twice a day. Cavaliers are not terribly different from other breeds except for their size. Providing kibbles especially made for small-breed dogs is highly recommended because they are made in smaller pieces and will be easier for them to chew and swallow.

Cavaliers of normal size for the breed are usually fed approximately one cup of kibble per day. This amount is certainly not set in stone, however, and will differ based upon the dog's weight and level of activity. Watch your Cavalier's weight carefully, and at the first sign of a weight problem (underweight or overweight), change the amount you are feeding. Also change his food if you notice digestive upsets or allergies.

Feeding Your Cavalier Senior

As your Cavalier ages, his eating habits and food preferences may well change. A constant monitoring of his weight will help to prevent the weight problems that many older dogs experience as their level of activity decreases and their metabolism slows. Also,

Your Cavalier's dietary needs will change as he ages.

your dog's teeth might be inadequate to chew the same types of foods that he ate in his youth. Painful teeth or gums can make mealtime unpleasant for him. Try feeding softer foods. Your Cavalier's senses may become duller with age, too, so his food will smell and taste less appetizing to him. If he becomes a picky eater, try warming his food to give it a more tantalizing aroma or separating it into smaller meals offered several times a day. Sometimes a change in routine will entice a fussy eater to pay more attention to his food.

Seniors will thrive on a lower percentage of protein now. Commercial foods for older dogs are manufactured with this in mind. These formulas also contain less fat and added nutrients like glucosamine and chondroitin to regenerate cartilage growth in the joints. Check food labels.

Your Cavalier should see the vet at least once a year so that she can assist you in determining the correct weight for your dog, as well as giving his teeth a complete exam. If a cleaning is required, your vet will schedule time for that since it is usually done under anesthesia. Be open to change as your dog changes with age.

FOOD-RELATED PROBLEMS

Dogs can have a variety of food-related problems, just as their humans can. Aside from weight gain and digestive upsets, foods can also cause allergies in dogs. In fact, food allergies often create the greatest need to change from one diet to another.

Food Allergies

Humans and dogs do not react to allergies in the same way. Humans tend to sneeze and have reddened eyes and runny noses. When a dog has an allergy, however, it is not likely that you will see sneezing or runny noses. You will most likely see scratching or excessive licking. He may lick his feet or other parts of his body until he has literally licked the skin right off! Before we can best understand how to "fix" an allergy issue, we probably should understand what an allergy is.

Allergy Symptoms

An allergy is a reaction to substances that induce hypersensitive reactions in both humans and animals. The substances that cause these reactions are called allergens. Allergens can enter the body in a number of ways, and what's worse, each exposure to an allergen will cause a stronger allergic reaction next time around. Allergens can be ingested, injected, or simply just touched. Besides food, dogs can be allergic to plastic, fabrics, and especially to antibiotics which are applied to the skin. If your dog is scratching, rubbing his face on the carpeting or other surfaces, licking his paws, or has watery

Loss of appetite or unexplained weight loss can be an indication of a serious health problem, so take your dog to the vet for a checkup.

eyes, these may very well be symptoms of an allergic reaction to foods or things in his environment.

Allergies tend to develop at some point between 1 and 4 years of age. Although there appears to be a genetic predisposition to them (if parents have them, offspring may develop them as well), they can also develop with no family history at all. All breeds are equally susceptible, as are mixed breeds. In Cavaliers, one of the most common signs of an allergic reaction is foot licking. If you do not actually see your dog licking his feet, you will know an allergic reaction is occurring if the white fur on his feet becomes pink in color.

Common Food Culprits

Corn and chicken are frequent causes of food allergies, but there are several other culprits such as proteins in milk, soy, beef, and pork. If your dog is allergy prone, you will need to carefully select a food that will not cause sensitivities that will aggravate him.

Often, feeding a good-quality premium or natural dog food and using a fatty acid supplement, such as one containing omega-3 fatty acids, will reduce inflammation and other symptoms of allergies.

Diarrhea and Constipation

Diets are often the main cause of both diarrhea and constipation. The key to both conditions is the lack of water or the lack of water removal. In the case of diarrhea, the large intestine is often not removing enough water from the food source, so the stool becomes very watery and hard to control. In this case, you may need to add foods or medication supplements that will help to absorb some of the water. In the case of constipation, there isn't enough water in the digestive system, so the stool becomes dry and much harder to pass. In either case, it is the unbalance of water and food wastes that creates the problems. Of the two, diarrhea is the most visible and the most dangerous. Constipation can cause a loss of appetite with subsequent possible dehydration, but diarrhea can cause dehydration very quickly and can be a killer, particularly for puppies.

Water-soluble fiber is very useful in treating both diarrhea and constipation. It will absorb water in the large intestine, slowing down the passage of waste products out of the body. It will also help to solidify waste products and can put an end to diarrhea. However, water-soluble fiber can also absorb water in the digestive tract thus helping dry, hard stool to become softer, with more bulk, and thus easier to pass. One of the most available food sources of high water-soluble fiber is plain canned pumpkin. Not pumpkin pie mix, which contains sugar and spices, but plain canned pumpkin. Adding one teaspoon to the meal of a small dog, or up to two or three tablespoons to the meal of a large dog, will do a lot to absorb water and thus help correct diarrhea and constipation.

Food Allergy Symptoms

Dogs can have a variety of food-related problems just as their humans can. If your Cavalier is biting or licking at his paws or his body, especially at the base of the tail, he may be allergic to something in his food. Check with your veterinarian to rule out any other possible causes, and then examine the label on your dog's food. If the main grain is corn, try a food with wheat or rice. If the main protein is chicken, switch to lamb. Try a food with lower fat or protein. If these changes don't eliminate the problem, talk to your veterinarian about offering your dog special foods made to deal specifically with these concerns.

Another easy way to treat constipation is to simply give your dog more water. If he doesn't appear to be drinking enough, add warm water to his kibble and allow it to soften before feeding it to him. He's still getting the water he needs, although it doesn't show in the food dish. Adding broth to kibble is another way to increase your dog's fluid intake, but broth usually contains quite a lot of sodium, so isn't useful for dogs who are on a low-sodium diet. Dogs will often eat ice chips and ice cubes when they have refused water, which is certainly worth a try. If your dog has somewhat of a sweet tooth, you can consider preparing a bowl of sugar-free gelatin for him to see if that will increase his appetite for water. Never use over-the-counter medications intended for humans; the ingredients may not be formulated for dogs and can create additional health issues.

Remember that dogs fed a raw diet (with its large water content) will consume much less water than dogs that are fed kibble, so be sure to make allowances for that.

Obesity

Obesity is a serious problem that can affect humans and dogs alike. Cavaliers seem to be especially prone to being overweight, partly due to their great love and appreciation for all things culinary, as we've already discussed, and partly due to their devotion to their owners; wanting to always be near them, they are not as physically active as many other breeds. So, unless you are reasonably active, chances are your Cavalier will turn into a couch potato. To prevent this, schedule regular times for walks, runs at a dog park, or sessions of fetch in the backyard. If your Cavalier is overweight, a weight-reducing diet combined with increased physical activity will help him to shed those extra pounds. Kibbles that are specially designed for the control of obesity will do more harm than good because they often contain fillers such as ground peanut shells. It is best to cut the amount that you are feeding and substitute the volume with healthy, low-calorie substitutes.

How to Tell If Your Dog Is Overweight

A dog is considered to be overweight if he weighs 20 to 25 percent more than the ideal weight for his breed and size. Being more than 30 percent of his ideal body weight means he is obese. Healthy Cavaliers should weigh between 13 and 20 pounds (6 and 9 kg).

You should be able to both see and feel if your Cavalier is overweight. From the side, you should see a slight "tuck-up" of the abdomen right behind the rib cage. From a standing position over your dog, you should see a visible waistline. With your hands on him, you should be able to feel each rib. Fat often deposits over the lower back, near the tail, and over the ribs.

Overweight Cavaliers are at risk for several chronic conditions such as heart disease, degenerative joint disease, and diabetes. Being overweight will also zap a dog's energy level and turn him into a full-time couch potato. These are obviously all good reasons to make sure your favorite canine friend eats properly.

EATING FOR LIFE

Feeding your Cavalier is not really as hard as it sounds. Your puppy will grow in appropriate growth patterns, your adult dog will thrive, and your elderly dog will live a longer and happier life—all benefits from feeding your dog the best possible diet for his life stage. You'll have to make lots of informed decisions based on your past experience with dogs, things you have read or learned from your breeder, your finances, your time and work schedules, and your own personal lifestyle preferences. Even storage space within your home will play a part in your decision-making.

Probably the most important thing to remember is that dogs have been the companions of humans since they shared a camp fire and a cave. Obviously, we've been doing something right because they are still our best friends. Our choices of food and the habitats with which we have provided them have also appeared to work out well. But this doesn't mean that responsible owners don't want to continue doing right by their canine pals, and many want to give them the best lives possible, which includes optimal nutrition. The best indication of whether your food choices and feeding schedule are appropriate for your Cavalier will be your dog. If he is active, healthy, has a good appetite, and is at the weight most appropriate for him, then you have fed him successfully.

5

GROOMING

Your Cavalier King Charles Spaniel

Everybody appreciates a Cavalier who looks beautiful, smells fresh, and isn't shedding excessively on clothes and furniture. With time and the right equipment and supplies, it is not very difficult to groom your dog. Even a quick comb through each day will prevent matting and help to keep the coat healthy.

Grooming generally refers to brushing, combing, shampooing, and nail care, but can also refer to trimming by professional groomers. How your dog is groomed will depend on whether or not you plan to show him. The American Kennel Club (AKC) breed standard for Cavaliers requires that they be shown in their natural state, with all of the feathering intact. However, pet owners are under no such ruling. They are free to trim their dogs as desired. A good dog groomer can give you several options for trimming, but you should be able to maintain the coat, nails, and ears at home with only a minimal outlay of time.

There's another reason for grooming, though, and that's to help keep your Cavalier healthy. Grooming frees the coat of dirt and grime and helps spread skin oils evenly throughout the coat. It also alerts you to small problems that can grow to be big problems if undetected, such as fleas, ticks, or any unusual skin growths.

In addition to keeping your dog clean, a grooming session can help you bond with your dog. Cavaliers love being with their pet parents, so your dog will love this special time he gets to spend with you.

PUPPY GROOMING

As soon as you bring your new puppy home, begin his grooming routine. The grooming needs of a puppy are very small compared with those of an adult, but this important time spent together can benefit both of you. Regular grooming gives you an opportunity to check your dog's skin, ears, and eyes. It is also your chance to give him a once over and a basic health check. If possible, have a grooming session at least one or two times per month, or more often if you desire.

Puppies begin to lose their puppy coats at five months or so. Their coats may be somewhat fluffy or flat, but the pigment on the chestnut-colored hair is significantly lighter than it will be on an adult Cavalier. In contrast, tricolor puppies are born with the darkest of blacks in their coats, and that won't change as the puppy loses his coat. As the adult Cavalier coat comes in on Blenheim and ruby types, you will notice a difference in the color as well. Whether the puppy coat was fluffy or flat, the adult coats all come in flat. Puppy coats aren't very long, and they rarely mat or tangle. All that is needed to maintain them is a regular brushing or combing, and shampooing and conditioning followed by a drying and combing as needed. Occasional baths do not harm your puppy as long as you are using quality products specifically made for dogs. The nails should be trimmed every two to three weeks (see nail trimming section).

Bath Training

If you begin bath training while your Cavalier is a puppy, he will grow comfortable with it by the time he reaches adulthood. You can get him used to the idea by placing him in a dry tub or sink. Next, give him a treat, praise him, and pet him gently. If he struggles to get out, hold him there but talk to him quietly to

In addition to keeping your dog clean and healthy, a grooming session offers you a great opportunity to bond with him.

reassure him. When he calms down, take him out of the tub. At this point, don't reward him or make a fuss over him—you want him to learn that he gets rewards for being in the tub, not for getting out. Repeat this process once a day for awhile, slowly increasing the time he remains in the tub. When he's comfortable in a dry tub, add a little lukewarm water so he gets his feet wet, and continue to reward him while he stays in the tub. When he accepts this, wet his body with lukewarm water from a sprayer or by pouring water onto him with an unbreakable container, again rewarding him for accepting it. Eventually, you'll have a dog who accepts bath time without fear and who may even enjoy being bathed.

Preparing for Bath Time

To prepare to bathe your puppy, place him on a grooming table or a nonslip surface that is at a comfortable height for both you and your dog. If you don't wish to invest in a grooming table, any countertop will do as long as it does not have a slippery surface. While your puppy is on the table or countertop, gently comb out all the mats that you may find. Puppies do not usually mat badly, but if mats are present they can usually be found behind the ears and on the rear legs. After the combing is completed, check the nails, and if they need trimming, trim them gently.

Bathing a Puppy

Now your puppy is ready for his bath. A Cavalier is small enough to fit neatly within a kitchen sink or bathtub. Apartment dwellers can easily use a shower that has a hand-held shower head, but make sure you place a rubber mat in the tub to prevent your dog from slipping and becoming injured. An inexpensive and handy way to bathe your Cavalier in a shower stall is to create a makeshift grooming table using one or two extra-large plastic storage containers that come with a tightly fitted lid. Determine how many you will need by the height that works best. Also, buy one or two smaller boxes to store your grooming and bathing apparatus. After the shower, the boxes can be stored in a closet or garage.

Before bringing your dog to his bath, have all of your supplies set up and ready to go. Put the stacked plastic box or boxes into the shower stall with a towel over the top to provide a nonslip surface and have your grooming products nearby.

Bath Time Checklist

Before bringing your dog to his bath, have all of your supplies set up and ready to go. After all, you can't expect your soapy dog to wait in the tub while you run downstairs for towels. Here's what you need:

- dog shampoo and conditioner
- cotton balls (placing a cotton ball in the opening of your dog's ears will help keep water out)
- ophthalmic ointment (placing an ointment in your dog's eyes prior to bathing will protect them from irritating shampoo and water)
- nonslip mat
- a hose or unbreakable container for rinsing
- one or two towels
- hair catcher for the drain

To begin, place your puppy in the sink, tub, or shower. Wet him with lukewarm water, apply shampoo, and gently work it into the coat with your fingers, beginning at the neck and working down to the tail. Be careful not to allow soap to enter his little ears or eyes. Once the puppy is bathed, rinse him thoroughly, and then blow him dry or towel him dry right away. Puppies chill easily, and you need to be prepared to warm him quickly.

Coat Check

If your puppy begins to scratch excessively or bite at irritated places on his skin, change the shampoos and conditioners you are using immediately. These activities are often a sign of an allergy to the products being used. However, these same activities are also frequently a sign of parasite infestation. Thoroughly examine your puppy for fleas, and if you find either fleas or "flea dirt" (dark specks left behind by feeding fleas), seek your vet's advice for the most age-appropriate and effective treatment. If your Cavalier puppy appears to have dandruff, take him to the vet for a skin scraping to check for mites. Although all dogs scratch from time to time, excessive scratching or biting at irritated spots on the fur should alert you to a possible problem. For the comfort of your dog, seek professional advice.

GROOMING THE ADULT CAVALIER

Cavaliers are said to have a single coat, which means that they do not produce the dense type of undercoat that breeds like Huskies and German Shepherds do. Some of them do not produce an undercoat at all, but most adult Cavaliers will produce at least a small amount of undercoat. This undercoat needs to be removed, or combed out, during grooming because the fuzzier texture of the undercoat leads to matting and tangling, particularly behind the ears and in the long feathering. Many tools are designed to remove the undercoat, but the best of all is a fine-toothed metal comb, which will gently remove it without cutting or damaging the outer coat.

How to Groom

Grooming an adult is much like grooming a puppy, but with much more dog to work on. Begin the grooming session by standing your Cavalier on a grooming table or countertop covered by a nonslip surface.

Next, check the entire coat for mats that need detangling. Comb gently through the coat using a fine-toothed comb. After you have combed through the body fur, move on to the head. Starting at the top of the ears, work the comb gently through the fur, being careful not to touch the eyes. If mats are to be found, they are usually located at the small pocket under the ear where the ear connects into the neck, although they can be found on the surface of the ear or the underside of the ear as well. If the fur is matted there, it will need to be combed out gently, working the tines of the comb into the fur at the edges of the mat.

Detangling products can be very useful in making a grooming session more comfortable for your dog. If you choose to use a detangling product, spray it on the mat and use your fingertips to work the product through it before attempting to use the comb. Once the mat has been removed, use the smaller fine-toothed comb to remove the remainder of the fuzzy undercoat from around the mat. Be vigorous in the removal of any undercoat in this area. If your Cavalier consistently develops matting around the ears, take him in for a vet check to rule out infection or parasites. Continue on to the other ear and then move on to the bib, the fur at the throat and neck.

On younger dogs, the bib rarely mats, but on older animals the mats under the throat area can be quite large and dense. If your dog is developing a lot of matting at the bib, consider removing his collar or any tags that dangle in front of it. Metal rabies and licensing tags can cause a grayish discoloration of the fur at the bib, and collars that cause the dog discomfort and scratching can lead to matting at the bib area. Using the fine-toothed comb, gently comb through the bib until the comb can be brought through the entire area without catching on either mats or undercoat.

As you proceed along the body, use your hands to feel under the arm pits and through the long feathering on the feet and legs. If the mats can be removed using a detangler and a comb, simply remove them. If they are too deeply matted, it may be more comfortable for the dog to have them cut out using blunt-tip scissors with caution. Of course, if you are showing your dog, you will not want to cut the coat—even a single hair of feathering is valuable to a show dog.

Regular grooming helps prevent mats, particularly behind the ears and on the long feathering of a Cavalier's coat.

Grooming Supplies

Proper grooming depends on having the right supplies. Here are some essentials:

- rubber curry comb for cleaning the coat and removing loose hairs
- soft bristle brush for finishing and polishing the coat
- nail clippers or nail grinder
- mild shampoo formulated for dogs
- doggy tooth care products

Next, turn up the feet and check the pads of each foot. Trim the hair between the pads, exposing the surface of the foot pads. This allows your dog to have better traction and a safer, more comfortable walk. It also fosters good hygiene in the feet. Check between the pads for any sharp objects that may be causing discomfort. The undersides of the feet may be trimmed with small electric clippers or blunt-tip scissors. You may trim the nails at this time (see nail trimming section). After the feet and legs have been combed through and the pads of the feet have been trimmed, it is time to move on to the abdomen and the hind legs.

The rear legs are another frequent location of matting on Cavaliers, especially the area going down the rear legs within the long feathering found on the outer surface of the hind legs. Even puppies can form mats there. The skin on the back legs is very sensitive, and removal of mats from that area can be both difficult and painful for your dog. It is far better to prevent the mats from forming by running your hands and fingers through the coat daily and working on small problem areas as they form. If your Cavalier is not going to be shown, there is no reason why you can't take him to a groomer from time to time to clip the hair on his legs down to prevent matting.

BATHING AN ADULT

Once all of the fur has been examined and every mat has been removed, you are ready to begin the bath. Any good-quality shampoo and conditioner that is formulated for use on dogs is sufficient, but some are definitely better than others. Experiment to see which products you and your dog prefer. You can also get some recommendations from your vet or groomer.

Again, bathing an adult is not unlike bathing a puppy, although you will want to invest more time because of his larger size and adult coat. To begin, wet your dog from head to toe with warm water; it should feel slightly cooler than you would prefer for your own bath. Avoid using very warm water because it not only can cause your dog pain but can be instrumental in removing too many of the essential skin oils. Apply shampoo and work up a generous lather, paying special attention to the undersides of the ears, which can get particularly oily. Using a washcloth only, gently lather the face and top of the head. Do not apply shampoo too close to the eyes. If you accidentally get shampoo in your dog's eyes, immediately rinse it with copious amounts of cool water. Follow that with a liberal flooding of the eye using regular saline solution such as the type purchased for use by contact lens wearers. Move from head to tail, lathering the shampoo as you go.

When you're done, rinse the shampoo out of the coat completely. Rinsing is important because any shampoo left behind can dry and damage your dog's skin. Follow with a good-quality conditioner and a second complete rinse.

Nail care keeps your dog's feet healthy. Gradually introduce nail trimming to your Cavalier when he's a puppy so that he can become accustomed to the process.

Towel your dog briskly for a few moments. Run a fine-toothed comb through the coat to get all of the hairs in the right direction, and begin blow drying at the ears. The blow dryer should be set on a medium or low setting, never on high. Hold the blow dryer several inches (cm) away from your dog's body and avoid his eyes. Blow dry your dog from front to back until he is completely dry, brushing the coat gently with a pin brush as you go.

NAIL TRIMMING

Long nails can make it hard for a dog to walk comfortably, and very long nails can curl around and puncture paw pads. If you walk your Cavalier regularly on rough pavement, you may never need to trim his nails. But if he spends most of his time in the house or in the yard, you'll need to trim his nails once a week or once every two weeks. Nail care is important, so get your dog used to the idea by handling his feet when he's a puppy. Hold a foot and play with the toes, then give him a treat. If you find you are too nervous to trim your dog's nails, take him to a groomer or a vet.

How to Trim Nails

If you're using nail clippers, cut the tip of the nail off, right where the nail starts to curve. If your dog has white nails, it is easy to see the "quick," the blood vessels inside the nail. The nails should be trimmed to the quick but not past the point where blood vessels are visible. On whole colors, the nails are black, so it will be difficult to see the quick.

Trim the nail to the beginning of the curve of the nail. If the nail bleeds after trimming, dip it into styptic powder and the bleeding should stop quickly. Pay careful attention to the dew claw, which is found on the front foot and corresponds to the location of the human thumb. Many breeders remove the dew claw when the puppy is only a few days old, but if it is left on your Cavalier, it will require regular trimming. Left untended, dew claws can curve and grow into the foot.

Many tools are available to trim your pet's nails. Look at several types and then pick one that you think will work the best for you and your dog.

EAR CARE

Because Cavaliers have long ears that hang over the opening of

To keep your Cavalier's ears healthy and well groomed, make a thorough inspection of them a weekly habit.

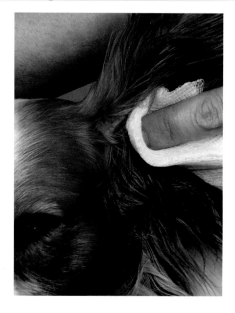

the ear canal, they probably have more than their fair share of ear problems. This is because air is unable to circulate, which creates a moist climate that is a perfect breeding ground for infectious organisms. Regular and careful examination of the ears is necessary to prevent ear diseases. Preventative care is also essential.

To keep your Cavalier's ears healthy and well groomed, make sure fur on the outside of the ear remains mat-free through frequent brushing and combing. Also make an inspection of the inside of the ear a weekly habit. Clean out the ear with a cotton ball or soft cloth soaked in ear cleanser. A healthy ear should be light pink. There should be no discharge and no odor. Again, if your dog is scratching and digging at his ear, tilting his head sideways, or if the ear is red, inflamed, or has a smelly discharge, take him to the vet for treatment.

EYE CARE

In general, a dog's eyes don't require much grooming. They should be clear and bright, and there shouldn't be any signs of discharge or swelling. However, because Cavaliers have large, prominent eyes, they often have small issues with pinkish staining on the fur under the eyes; this is caused by a variety of things. Allergies to various environmental agents can cause it, as well tear ducts that do not function sufficiently to carry tears away from the surface of the eyes. Teething puppies also develop staining; irritation to the gums will often cause chronic tearing because of the slight discomfort to the area under the eyes. This usually disappears after 1 year of age. Several commercially available eye stain removers are on the market; these can be found in pet catalogues and pet supply stores. You can also use plain witch hazel, which is available at any drug store. Almost any product will work equally well, and they are all considered to be safe for the dog as long as you avoid getting the solution into the eye.

To remove eye staining, saturate a cotton ball with your chosen product. Using a gentle circular motion, wipe the stained area. Rub lightly with a slight scrubbing action, and take care not to allow the product or the cotton ball to touch the surface of the eye. Next, rinse the area with plain warm water.

Although you may only schedule a bath for your Cavalier every few weeks, you may want to perform this eye cleaning routine daily. Eye stains are not only disfiguring, but they can also be annoying if they begin to produce odor. The odor is caused by bacterial growth when the fur under the eye stays moist all the time; the skin provides the warm environment necessary for bacterial or fungal growth. The combination of moisture and bacterial/fungal growth will often create an odor much like that of mildewed laundry. Regular use of the product you have chosen will prevent odor and can slowly work to remove the stain.

DENTAL CARE

Keeping your dog's teeth clean should be part of your grooming routine. Aside from keeping his breath fresh, regularly brushing your Cavalier's teeth can guard against health problems because plaque can build up and eventually harden into tartar that continues to collect on tooth surfaces. Tartar causes gum abscesses, and bacteria from those abscesses can circulate through your dog's blood system causing heart, liver, or kidney problems.

Examine your dog's teeth frequently, especially the teeth of a new puppy. Cavaliers will often retain a baby canine tooth, which will be firmly planted next to the adult canine. The baby canine needs to be removed if it doesn't come out by itself because it will cause a variety of problems for your dog.

How to Brush

Start brushing your Cavalier's teeth when he is a puppy. By getting him used to the routine while he is young, he will not make a big fuss over it later on. If you can brush his teeth every day, great. If not, try to do it two or three times a week. Of course, continue this routine when your dog is an adult as well.

To begin getting your dog used to brushing, wrap your finger in gauze and rub it over his teeth and gums. Use a dab of flavored toothpaste made for pets; these come in meaty flavors that your dog will enjoy. Never use toothpaste made for humans; they are too foamy, and the added fluoride is not good for your dog. Once your dog accepts this, you can advance to a doggy toothbrush.

While cleaning your dog's teeth, take note of any problems that may need attention. If he has bad breath or it smells differently, he may have a problem with his teeth. Broken or cracked teeth will also need attention.

Regularly scheduled dental appointments with your vet are extremely important because tooth decay and dental infections have been implicated in so many diseases. Cardiac disease and infertility and sterility are thought to have a connection with bad oral hygiene. If you show your dog, he must have all of his teeth because he will be showing them to a vet at every show. Be aware that the dental cleaning done by your vet will probably require anesthesia, although some vet techs can scale the teeth of almost any dog without anesthesia. These services are often offered at dog shows and are well worth searching out in your area.

Be very conscientious about your dog's dental care. A diet of high-quality dry dog food can help slow the formation of plaque, and some companies now offer special foods that are supposed to help prevent plaque. Nylabone chew toys and dental devices, as well as raw or sterilized beef bones, may also help.

Doggy Bad Breath

If your dog has very bad breath, check his teeth and gums, as well as the pockets between his cheeks and gums. Dental infections and tooth decay can lead to bad breath. A change in food can frequently help to alleviate objectionable breath. The addition of chew bones made of polyurethane can make a significant difference. Toys with rough, textured surfaces, will also help to remove plaque as well as massage the gum surfaces. Brushing teeth daily is a good practice and can ensure that bad doggy breath doesn't reoccur.

GROOMING FOR A SHOW

The grooming routine for a show dog is only slightly different from that of a pet, but those differences are important. When a show dog walks into the ring, the first thing that registers with onlookers is the beautiful, healthy coat. A show dog's coat must be kept in meticulous condition. Of utmost importance for Cavaliers is maintaining a stain-free coat and well-groomed ears.

Coat Stain Removal

Particolor Cavaliers usually have white feet and legs, and a white abdomen, bib, and tail. It is not unusual for these white areas to become stained over time. Saliva will stain them a shade of pink, and grass, soil, and exposure to garden areas containing bark will also stain the coat. For some reason, some dogs are subject to staining much more than others. It's possible that the hair itself differs in some way to make these coats more susceptible, perhaps because the hair shaft is more porous. Whatever causes it and however it gets there, staining is difficult to remove.

Cavalier coats cannot be bleached or artificially lightened. Because the breed standard is so specific about this, it falls to the Cavalier breeder to locate the best products for simple stain removal. Some very good products are available that will remove stains and keep the coat in wonderful show condition. When used as directed at every grooming, they will keep your Cavalier's coat in great condition and glistening white.

Grooming the Ears for Showing

The long and luxurious ears of the Cavalier are certainly his crowning glory. The care they require for showing takes a little extra effort. Being single-coated dogs, most Cavaliers produce an undercoat of sorts that is evident on the ears. Whereas pet owners are well advised to remove the undercoat from the ears because it contributes significantly to matting, my recommendation is that exhibitors leave every hair on the ears. It is this soft, fuzzy undercoat that gives the ear its fullness.

When bathing and grooming your Cavalier for a dog show, shampoo the ears at least twice using a liquid dish soap that contains a degreasing component. Dawn liquid dish soap works

A show dog's coat must be kept in meticulous condition. If you decide to show your Cavalier, he also will have to be groomed to conform to the breed standard.

extremely well and is approved by many vets. Both the inner and outer aspect of the ear flap often gets oily because of continued contact with our hands. This oil must be completely removed in order for the ears to show well. The use of a degreasing soap will help to remove all oil. If your are showing, do not condition the ears. Conditioner, while not an oily product, can still weigh down the hair on the ears and prevent them from attaining their maximum fullness.

Carefully towel the ears dry before you begin working with the blow dryer. Begin blowing the ears and brushing them with a pin brush at the same time. Blow dry them until each individual hair is separate and bone dry. Dry both the inner and outer aspects of the ear completely. Then dry the fur around the ear and on the neck completely. After they have dried, you will notice that the degreasing soap, together with the lengthy period of blow drying, has resulted in a very full, lush-looking ear. This is the look that you are seeking. Preserve each hair, degrease the fur on the ears, and blow dry the ears until each individual hair is perfectly dry. Practice this on regular grooming days so that you feel confident on show day.

Grooming as a Health Check

In addition to making your dog look good, grooming time is also an opportunity to do a health check. Before you begin grooming, take a minute and run your hands up and down your dog's body. Notice if he has any sensitive areas, lumps, bumps, scratches, or sores.

Part his fur in a few places and check for signs of fleas or ticks. Take a look at his coat. It should be shiny, and there should be no missing patches of fur. The skin shouldn't be very dry or flaky, and the fur shouldn't be brittle. Check the feet and look for cracked foot pads or overgrown/ingrown nails.

Look inside the ears and check for excessive ear wax buildup or signs of ear mites. Open your dog's mouth and examine his teeth and gums. The gums should be pink and healthy, and there should be no missing or broken teeth. The eyes and nose should be clean and clear, not runny.

Taking a few extra minutes to examine your dog before you groom him keeps him healthy and alerts you to any physical changes that may indicate a problem.

Products for Grooming

Many products are available for grooming your Cavalier. Probably the most reasonable prices can be found in the various pet supply stores. It is also easy to order supplies by phone or online. Many companies will send you catalogues if you call and request them. Anything that you will need for grooming or showing your dog is readily available.

Grooming Table

You may want to invest in a grooming table. If you buy one, you will also need a restraint to hold your dog firmly and safely in place as you groom him; these sometimes come with the tables. Cavaliers do nicely on a small- or medium-size grooming table. It can also double as a training table to prepare a show puppy for his career as you teach him to stand for the judge's exam.

Other Supplies

If you are grooming for the show ring, you will need a variety of supplies. Combs and brushes of different sizes and types are necessary. You'll need a nail trimmer as well. Look at several types before buying one. Check the hand fit on several different models to make sure you are purchasing one that you are comfortable using because they last for several years with proper care. You may want to consider purchasing a small pair of electric clippers for use on the bottom of the feet. The hair between the pads requires trimming, and it is often more convenient and faster to use an electric clipper. You will only need a small pair because the feet are the only area that can be trimmed, according to the breed standard.

Of course, you will want to purchase a variety of dog shampoos and conditioners for everyday use, show day use, and other special needs as they arise. Plan to purchase a blow dryer specifically made for use with dogs. Again, shop the catalogues for prices and styles.

CHOOSING A PROFESSIONAL GROOMER

There may be times when your Cavalier needs to be groomed and you'd rather not do it yourself. Seeking the services of a professional groomer can solve that problem. To find a good, reliable groomer, ask your veterinarian, family, and friends for

If you'd rather not groom your dog yourself, seek the services of a professional groomer.

recommendations. Most groomers are kind and gentle with dogs, but it's always best to get referrals. It also helps to know what to look for when choosing one. Here are some questions to ask:

- What training and experience do the groomers in the shop have?
- What kind of shampoos and conditioners do they use? What other products do they use on your breed?
- Do they use a hand-held drier or cage drier? If a cage drier, how often do they check your dog? Is someone always present when the dog is exposed to the drier?
- Do they clean the ears?
- Do they check, and if necessary, express the anal glands?
- Do they use sedatives? If so, who sedates and monitors the pet? What training have they had in the safe use of sedatives and in first aid? What will they do if something goes wrong?
- How long will your dog need to be there? Where will he be

kept when he's not being groomed? Where will he be taken to potty? Is the area fenced?

- What are the normal fees for a Cavalier, and what is included in that fee?

The facilities should be tidy and clean, and dogs who aren't being groomed should be housed in secure, reasonably comfortable cages or crates with access to drinking water. Equipment such as scissors, combs, brushes, clippers, and grooming tables should be disinfected between dogs. If you don't feel comfortable about a groomer, don't leave your dog with that establishment. Trust your instincts, and don't be polite at the expense of your peace of mind or your dog's well-being.

BONDING TIME

Grooming your Cavalier can be fun. With proper preparation and training beginning in puppyhood, your dog will learn to look forward to bath time as bonding time with you. And by maintaining a regular schedule of grooming, you will also make sure your dog is healthy by being alerted to problems early. All of these things make the grooming time spent with your Cavalier rewarding for both you and your dog.

Chapter

6

TRAINING *and* BEHAVIOR
of Your Cavalier King Charles Spaniel

A ll dog owners love a well-behaved dog, and even those few people in the world who haven't fallen in love with dogs will be able to tolerate one who has been taught how to behave when asked to do so. Cavaliers can be trained to do a wide variety of things, from simple basic obedience to agility trials. Problem behaviors can also be addressed by good training techniques. Dogs may appear to fall into habits that are problematic for us, but are perfectly normal and instinctual for them. With training, you can manage those behaviors and live comfortably together. The key to loving every day that you live with your Cavalier is to teach him to do the things you need him to do and train him to stop doing the things you don't want him to do. Sounds simple enough? Well, in many ways it is. It takes time, patience, and treats in your pocket, but it can be fun and rewarding.

WHY TRAIN YOUR CAVALIER?

All dogs need to learn boundaries. Cavaliers need to be trained for their safety, your comfort and convenience, and sometimes just to give them one more way to please you. Dogs who run out of every open door, don't come back to you when you call them, and jump on children and strangers are not usually as welcome in the neighborhood as well-behaved dogs. Training is important for so many reasons, but the main things to focus on are safety and good behavior.

POSITIVE TRAINING

Dogs love to please their owners, and they learn quickly and effectively when training is a pleasant experience. It doesn't take them long to understand that if they sit when they hear the word "sit," something good happens. They love receiving praise and especially love getting that favorite toy or small food treat. Dogs have a far more difficult time comprehending what is expected of them if they are struck or if voices are raised to them. They will associate training with unpleasant things and become very resistant. Make sure that all the training you do is positive, with rewards, praise, and treats. Never use punishment of any kind, whether it be physical, verbal, or psychological. You'll be happier for it, and your dog will learn quickly the things that are expected of him so that you can share a happy household.

BEFORE YOU BEGIN TRAINING

Before you begin the process of training your Cavalier puppy, or perhaps even before you bring him home, decide what it is that you expect from him. What are you hoping to accomplish with your puppy? What are your priorities? Almost anyone who contemplates this question comes to the same conclusion.

The first thing that you may be hoping to accomplish is getting your puppy housetrained. The second thing that is needed is to involve every member of the family in the training process. Consistency is going to be the key to making training effective, and every family member needs to be instructed as to what it is you are trying to do. Even a 2 year-old human child can see when a puppy is turning in circles and sniffing the carpet and can alert an adult that the puppy is engaging in "getting ready to potty" behavior. Children cannot train a Cavalier puppy alone, and they should not

Dogs love to please their owners, and they learn quickly and effectively when training is a positive experience.

be asked to do so, but they can certainly participate in the process. They can be taught never to take the puppy out of his crate without supervision. They can be taught never to strike or physically punish him, and they can be taught how to use the proper tone of voice to both reward and correct him. If the puppy is to be successfully trained to be a good citizen and a reliable member of the household, it will be necessary to engage the entire family in his training.

In the case of dog training, it does, indeed take a village. Studying dog training, reading books prior to the arrival of your puppy, and watching dog training videos can all be good family fun and help to build anticipation for the arrival of the new family member.

SOCIALIZATION

Most Cavalier puppies and adults are outgoing, friendly, fearless little dogs. Temperament is determined both by genetics and home environment. If a breeder has produced a Cavalier puppy who is a little bit shyer than is desirable for showing, that puppy will be homed as a pet. Any puppy can blossom in the right environment, provided that a careful and responsible owner gives him every opportunity to be properly socialized. Socialization is an important part of dog ownership, and it begins the day you bring home your new Cavalier.

How to Socialize Your Cavalier

Begin by providing your puppy with a safe and secure environment within his new home. Be sure that he has adequate areas in the house and outside in the yard for exploration and romping. If he feels safe and loved at home, you are laying the foundation for him to feel safe and secure in unfamiliar locations as well.

When your puppy is ready, take him out for a walk around the neighborhood or take him with you on short trips. Many retail stores welcome well-behaved puppies and dogs. Plan to keep your puppy in a shopping cart but cover the bottom with a piece of fabric so that his feet won't slip through. Do not plan to take him out on-lead until he is much older. While you are there, allow people to pet him and pay attention to him—even the shyest puppy will quickly respond to people who scratch his ears and give him attention. A Cavalier puppy attracts a great deal of attention wherever he goes, so be sure to take advantage of each trip you make away from home.

If you have children, walk them to their bus stops each day with the puppy on lead. Allow other children to pet him. Cavaliers want to meet and greet every new face, and socialization of this sort is invaluable. Your puppy needs exercise and walks every day anyway, so choose times during the week when you can turn a dog walk into a socialization exercise as well.

Walk your dog on lead in areas where he will be met by both people and other dogs. Always be mindful of his personal safety whenever another dog approaches. If an unknown dog comes forward with teeth bared and hackles raised, your puppy will not be able to comprehend that these behaviors represent body language used by dogs to ward off intruders. Quickly pick up your puppy and do not maintain eye contact with the threatening dog. Hopefully, his owner has him well under control, but you cannot trust the life of your Cavalier to a careless handler.

If you have determined that the dogs you are meeting are safe and well mannered, allow your Cavalier to greet them. These events are important parts of his socialization, and in a brief amount of time you will discover that the puppy who you once thought was shy has blossomed into an outgoing, fearless little dog living completely up to his breed standard. The key to successful socialization is frequent exposure to new and different people, animals, and experiences that end with a positive result. Your Cavalier is learning new things every day, and one of your responsibilities is to help him learn that the world is a fun and exciting place.

Early Socialization

Socialization begins the day you bring your new puppy home. Exposure to new people, places, and experiences will help ensure that your Cavalier is friendly and comfortable with everyone. An anxious, fearful dog is much more likely to bark excessively, have episodes of submissive urination, or even bite someone approaching him. Dogs react to unknowns with fear. Being introduced to a wide variety of people with different voices, mannerisms, clothing, etc. will pave the way toward having a well-socialized and fearless pet.

CRATE TRAINING

Dogs are clean animals by nature, and although they can't always control their bladder and bowels as young puppies, they do not like to soil their sleeping environment—it is their nature to keep their den clean. If a dog has learned to look upon his crate as his private little den, he will quickly revert to his instinct to keep it clean. A crate can help to simplify training, especially housetraining. If you have your puppy on a reasonable schedule, he soon will learn to hold it until he is taken outside. A crate also can keep your puppy confined and out of trouble when you can't

A crate is a useful tool when housetraining and traveling.

supervise him, as well as help you transport him when traveling.

Don't think of a crate as a "jail." Think of it as a cozy place where your dog feels safe and secure. A misconception prevails that placing a dog in a crate is an act of cruelty that deprives him of his freedom. A dog, like his ancestor the wolf, is a denning animal. His natural instinct is to have a private area to which he can retreat. As long as you never use the crate as a punishment, your dog will learn to associate it with positive activities. Also, dogs will develop a sense of safety in their own crates, and because they feel secure there they are less likely to suffer from separation anxiety when they are left alone for long periods of time.

Dogs who are left in closed crates during their owner's absence are safer than dogs who are left to roam about the house unsupervised. An unsupervised puppy can quickly find ways to get into trouble or get hurt. Crating your puppy or dog is a safety factor that should be addressed for his entire life.

Crate Location

Choose a location for the crate where your Cavalier can be close to family members. While he's a small puppy, you may want to have an additional crate in your bedroom.

Your puppy needs to be close enough to family members to

know they are nearby even though he is napping.

The crate itself provides all of the seclusion your Cavalier needs. Crates can be placed under end tables. Some very good-looking dog crates are available from many pet supply catalogues that are made of resin wicker and look nice in any living room or family room.

Appropriate Length of Confinement

Here are the times that a young pup can safely be confined:
- 9 to 10 weeks of age: 30 to 60 minutes
- 11 to 13 weeks of age: 1 to 3 hours
- 14 to 16 weeks of age: 3 to 4 hours
- over 16 weeks of age: 4 to 6 hours

How to Crate Train Your Cavalier

To introduce your Cavalier puppy to the crate, allow him to investigate it with the door open. Toss a small treat into the crate. When he follows, praise him. Let him come out for another small treat. Next time, toss the treat in the crate, and when he goes to get it, close the door for about 30 seconds. Praise him and repeat again, this time for about 30 seconds longer. This is a wonderful way to build his tolerance and get him used to being in the crate gradually.

Once he seems used to that, try placing him in the crate and walking out of the room. If he cries, ignore him. Don't keep going back to the crate and talking to him because you are then simply reinforcing the undesired behavior. Once he settles in, listen for him. As soon as you hear him crying (usually after he's taken a short nap), return to the crate, quickly pick him up, praise him, and take him outdoors immediately without allowing him any floor time. By the time he's an adult, he will have learned the word "crate" and will associate his crate time with patting, cuddling, praise, and treats.

Lengthy Stays in the Crate

If your puppy is going to be alone in his crate for more than three hours, purchase a small water dish that attaches to the interior of the crate. Do not leave food in the crate. Your puppy can be fed in the crate if necessary, but the food and food dish should be completely removed between meals. Feeding him in the crate will be of assistance to you as you housetrain him.

Your breeder may have already begun the process of crate training. A pup of even 10 weeks can manage to sleep through the night, as long as he was taken out the very last thing before going to bed and wasn't fed his last meal of the day after 4 or 5 pm or allowed to consume large amounts of water prior to being crated. It is completely acceptable to move the crate into your bedroom at night so that the puppy can see you and hear your reassuring voice.

HOUSETRAINING

Housetraining is the process of training your Cavalier to potty only when he is in an acceptable location. This can be a litter box, a puppy pad, or outdoors. It is difficult to live with a dog who consistently potties inside the house on carpeting and floors. Housetraining will make your dog a better companion to you. And a well-housetrained dog is welcomed by all.

Before You Begin

Before deciding on a housetraining technique, you must first assess your own personal situation with regard to housing and exits to the outdoors. If you are an apartment dweller, you may want to consider training your Cavalier to use a puppy pad or litter box. Believe it or not, small dogs can be trained to use a litter box, although they do not dig a hole for excrement and cover it up as cats do. If you live in a house, but it does not have a fenced yard, you'll need to housetrain your puppy to eliminate outdoors. This will involve teaching him to let you know that he needs to go outside, of course, but you will need to leash him to walk him outdoors. If your house has a fenced yard that is secure and safe for your puppy, you may want to consider teaching him how to use a dog door. These are easy to install and even come in models designed for use on sliding doors.

Housetraining Tools

Before you begin housetraining, make sure you have all of the necessary equipment already on hand. Reading a good book on the topic beforehand is always helpful.

First on your list of housetraining tools should, of course, be a kennel or similar type of dog crate. You'll also need a crate pad (or two) that fits neatly into the bottom of the crate. It's best to buy

Be Patient

Be prepared to be patient when housetraining a Cavalier puppy. Smaller dogs can be somewhat more difficult to train than larger dogs for a variety of reasons. For starters, their bladders are smaller and they simply can't hold it as long. Because their puddles are also small, we sometimes may not be as watchful as we would be if we were housetraining a Saint Bernard. Although Cavaliers of any age love a good long romp in the snow, they almost all hate rain and getting their feet wet, so if you live in a rainy climate you may need to consider providing a covered area for the dog's outside bathroom. Just be prepared for housetraining to take some time and remember that each puppy is an individual and will learn in his or her own time.

one especially made for the size crate that you have purchased. The pad should also be very durable and washable; washing pads often will prevent "doggy odor" near the area of your crate. Avoid using throw rugs because puppies will pull out the fibers of the rug and can possibly swallow them. Likewise, terry cloth towels do not make comfortable or safe crate pads. Fleece is a good fabric choice for a crate pad because it washes and dries quickly.

If your puppy develops the habit of relieving himself in his crate, consider putting him in a smaller crate, one that doesn't allow him as much room to move about, or remove his crate pad until the problem is resolved. Generally speaking, all dogs want their sleeping areas to be clean. If the crate is large enough that your puppy views it as an apartment with a bathroom versus a studio apartment, it may well be time to "size down" until the he learns how to keep his sleeping area clean.

The Potty Command

You have the equipment, you've decided where you will be taking your Cavalier to relieve himself, and you feel that you are ready to begin. Not quite! Hold your horses! There are still a few more things to do, like teaching a *potty* command. From day one, you'll need to use a single word or term to signal your

When housetraining your Cavalier, choose a spot in your yard where you want him to eliminate and take him to that same area every time.

puppy that it is time to potty. "Potty," or any other term that suits you, will work as long as you don't use the same word for another command, which will just confuse your dog. This specific command will let your Cavalier know that he has reached the correct place and it is time for him to go potty. You will also need a reward system of some sort. Think this over carefully because you will need to be very consistent both in the phrase or word that you use as his signal and the treat with which you reward him after he has done his business and is ready to return to the house.

Rewards

Cavaliers are such good-natured little dogs that they honestly do their best to please you. But sometimes there may be a little glitch in the system between their wanting to make you happy and their knowing *how* to make you happy. By rewarding your dog when he has behaved correctly, you can reinforce the desired response and avoid confusion during other training sessions. This is why it's a good idea to choose a reward system and stick to it.

Many Cavaliers can be motivated simply with verbal praise such as "Good boy!" or "Super job!" Other times they may need the addition of a reassuring touch, a pat, or a stroke. When housetraining, it isn't always necessary to utilize a food reward, although if it works for you to do so, do it immediately in response to the dog's relieving himself. As soon as he has completed emptying his bladder or bowel, say "Good Boy!" and quickly give him a small food treat or scratch his ears. Be sure not to let a lot of time (even a few seconds is a lot to a small dog) expire between the completion of the desired action and the reward. Give him the reward on the spot and instantly.

How to Housetrain Your Cavalier

Housetraining is essential in order for you and your family to enjoy time spent with your Cavalier. However, as discussed, there is more than one method of housetraining. Cavaliers can be crate trained or trained to go to the door; they can learn to tap on a hanging bell or even to use puppy pads inside the home. Whatever works best for your dog is, of course, your best option. The secret to housetraining is to have a schedule, take your puppy out frequently, be consistent, and until he is housetrained, never leave him loose unattended.

Outdoor Housetraining

Choose a spot in your yard where you want your puppy to go. Take him to that same area every time, and bring him out on a leash so that you can direct him to the correct spot. Once you get to the proper spot, encourage your puppy to go with the command you taught him earlier. Whatever phrase you choose, make sure that all family members use the same command. Eventually, your puppy will connect the phrase with the action.

Follow a schedule, and your puppy will soon learn to wait until he is taken out before he goes. Generally, take your puppy out after naps, after eating, and after play sessions. Carry him outside. Don't coax him to leave his crate and follow you through the house, because odds are he won't make it, and the fewer accidents he makes in the house, the faster the housetraining will go. Watch your puppy for signs that he needs to go. Some puppies will sniff and circle, but others will just squat and go, so pay attention.

If you take your puppy out at bedtime (around 11 pm), he should be okay until morning (around 6 am). Make sure that he has a nice warm bed, because if he gets cold during the night, he'll wake up, and if he wakes up, he'll need to go out. No matter where your puppy spends the day, let him sleep in a crate in someone's room so that if he does wake up, someone can take him out. Don't ignore his whining, or housetraining will take much longer.

Indoor Housetraining

You can use the fact that your new puppy or dog has a natural instinct not to soil his sleeping area to your advantage when housetraining him. As tempting as it is to let your new puppy nap on your lap as you watch TV, maintain the crate training you began earlier by reinforcing the crate as his sleeping area. He will bark when he wakes up to let you know that nap time is over and that he is ready to get out of his crate and potty.

Carry your puppy to the pottying location that you have chosen. Do not allow his feet to touch the floor. Remember, he can't hold it for long, and he will assume that the first accommodating place that you allow him to squat and urinate or defecate is the place you intend him to go. Carry him to the chosen potty location, whether it is on a pad or in a litter box. Place him down and use the verbal command that you have chosen. Once he has relieved himself, praise him and reward him with meal time or some play

Housetraining Preschool

If you bring your puppy home before he is 16 weeks of age or so, you may find that you will need to put a small fenced area around the crate and leave the door open so that he can leave the crate to relieve himself on puppy pads or in a litter box left within the enclosure. After 16 weeks, his little bladder is more reliable and you can begin his crate training in earnest.

time. Remember that within 15 to 30 minutes of eating he will begin searching for a convenient place to go potty again. For that reason, it is a good idea to feed him in his crate, and as soon as he has finished eating, pick him up and carry him to the chosen potty location again. Let him follow you back inside to play for a while. Practice this routine consistently.

Housetraining With a Bell

Another popular housetraining technique is to hang a bell near the door your puppy uses when he goes outdoors to potty. By using a small clicker, you can teach him to ring the bell with his nose, thus alerting you to the fact that he needs to go out. Clicker training is fun, and it is an easy way to help your dog learn to do the "right" thing.

Many dog trainers incorporate clicker training into their training methods. Clickers can be purchased at pet stores very inexpensively. The concept of clicker training isn't very complicated once you learn the basics. Here's how it works: Give your puppy a command. When he obeys the command, click immediately and give him a small reward—a treat of some kind works well. As your puppy responds more and more to the command, begin decreasing the number of food treats. Click after every positive reaction, but give a food treat only on every third response, and then gradually spread out the treats so that your dog eventually begins to understand that the click is his positive reinforcement. Puppies learn very quickly with this technique.

To train your puppy to ring the bell, play with him next to the bell. Touch the bell and waggle it in his face. As soon as his nose or paw touches the bell, quickly click and reward him with a small food treat. Immediately open the door and walk outdoors with him. Several sessions may be required, but eventually the puppy will learn that touching the bell is a good thing and that it will get the door open so he can go out to potty.

Dealing With Accidents

Never hit a puppy or rub his nose in his feces or urine, and never raise your voice. If the puppy has an accident in the house, chalk it up to inattention on your part and attribute it to the fact that you didn't act quickly enough to meet his needs. If you make fear of punishment the motivating factor behind housetraining

your puppy, it will take much longer to housetrain him, and it will be a much more traumatic event for both of you. It also teaches your puppy to make an association between being taught a new skill and being punished for not immediately accomplishing it. You will have much more luck with all types of training if you decide right from the start that you will reward your puppy for accomplishing his goal and ignore his mistakes and mishaps.

If your puppy has an accident in his crate, do not punish him. Simply clean the crate and then follow the cleaning with the use of an odor neutralizing solution available at most pet stores. Wash the crate pad and start over.

LEASH TRAINING

It is unlikely that the breeder has leash trained your puppy, although it is certainly a bonus. One of the easiest ways to leash train a puppy of any breed is to simply tether him to his mother and allow her to walk around the yard with the puppy tethered to her collar on a short lead. Puppies have a natural inclination to follow their moms, and moms have the patience to manage a rambunctious little puppy who wants to kick up his heels and run through the garden when she'd prefer to lie in the sun.

If your puppy has not come to you already leash trained, you

To teach your Cavalier to walk on leash, he must first learn to follow you.

will need to take him with you to a pet store for a fitting of a light-weight collar and leash. Cavaliers are small dogs, so training will be a more pleasant experience for all concerned if the training tools used, such as collars and leashes, are lightweight and fit well. Harnesses work well for small dogs as well.

How to Leash Train Your Cavalier

After you have purchased a leash and collar, begin leash training. Start by just attaching the collar and leash to your puppy and allowing him to walk around the house and yard with the leash following along behind. This activity must be supervised at all times so that he does not become entangled and hurt himself.

As soon as your puppy has begun to accept the leash following along behind him, tie it to an unmovable object in the yard or house. Your puppy will be surprised that he is no longer allowed to move about freely and may fight the feeling, but once he has caught on that he can't move the object, he will relax and slowly accept that he must stay where the leash and collar have placed him. The best thing about this part of the training is that *you* are not involved with restricting his freedom.

Once your puppy has begun to settle in and learns that his movements are restricted when he is on a leash and wearing a collar, it is time to practice walking him on leash. To get him to follow you, take the other end of the leash and call him in a positive, energetic way. If your puppy starts to pull back on the leash and demonstrates to you that he wishes to go in a different direction, simply sit down. Don't pull on the leash and don't use your voice as a discouragement or punishment. Simply sit down. Call the puppy to you using an encouraging, positive tone of voice. As he returns to you, praise him using the slightest amount of pressure pulling him toward you. Once he has reached you, praise him profusely, hold him, and scratch his ears or reward him with a food treat. Then get up and start again walking in the direction that you have chosen.

After doing this several times, your puppy will learn that if he wishes to explore, he must follow you. He will also learn that he will not be allowed to determine the direction of his walks. It will only take a day or two to get him walking correctly on leash once he understands this critical point. Remember, a Cavalier's entire temperament is wrapped around the concept of making you happy.

It is up to you to let him know what he needs to do in order for you to be pleased. Using a proper tone of voice, a loving touch, and food rewards will tell him when he has done the right thing.

On a separate note, some Cavalier owners leave a collar on their dog all the time. They feel doing this allows them to keep an easily seen identification tag on their pet. However, leaving a collar on at all times also presents a safety risk of sorts. It may be a small safety risk, but certainly one that needs consideration. A dog might get his collar snagged on a piece of furniture or even on an interior portion of his crate, which can lead to a choking accident or death. For your dog's protection, never leave his collar on when he is unsupervised.

BASIC TRAINING

Basic obedience involves teaching your dog to walk on a leash at your left side, sit at your left side automatically when you stop walking, sit on command at any location, lie down and stay down until you release him from that position, and come when you call him. Many Cavalier owners are content if their dog learns just the basics because these simple commands will result in a well-behaved pet who is a pleasure to be with wherever you go.

Heel and Sit

One of the most important commands your dog should be taught is the *sit* command. Along with teaching him to sit patiently, it can also be used to teach him not to jump on people.

How to Teach the Heel *and* Sit *Commands*

Because all dogs should know how to walk on your left side on leash (which is called "heeling"), it is best to combine the *sit* command with walking on your left side. Your Cavalier needs to learn how to sit quietly as you talk to neighbors, get the mail, or stop to watch something.

To begin, place your dog on your left side and start walking at a brisk pace. As you walk, give the *heel* command saying "Heel." If your dog hasn't been leash trained, he may resist the feeling of something around his neck at first. Gently pull him toward you and keep walking, talking to him as you go. Praise him and reach down and pat him from time to time if he stays next to you. Use the one-word *heel* command each time you begin walking.

As soon as he has accepted the feel of the leash and is

Sit is one of the easiest commands to teach a dog, and it is a good building block for learning other skills.

consistently walking next to your left side, begin teaching him the *sit* command. Begin by walking at a brisk pace, then stop, keeping him on a short leash so that he can't stray very far from your left side. Give him the command "Sit." At the same time, reach down and gently push his little rear end down until he is sitting, and immediately reward that behavior with a small treat. Praise him by saying "Good sit." Use a very positive and encouraging tone of voice so that your dog can tell that you are pleased by his correct response.

Next, resume walking at a brisk pace as if you fully expect your dog to follow and walk along at your left side. When he is walking next to you, stop again and give the same one-word command followed by gently pushing his little rear end down into the sit position. Reward him for his good performance. Repeat this until your dog sits automatically each time you stop walking.

When your dog is heeling and sitting whenever you stop, it is time to reinforce his understanding of the word "sit" by doing the training at home, off leash. Set aside a short period of time for training sessions each day. Use the same steps you used to train on leash. To begin, sit next to your puppy. Say the one-word command "Sit," and push his little rear end down. Then reward and praise him. Repeat this over and over until your dog has learned the command. You must remember to practice these commands often so that your dog doesn't forget them.

Stay

The *stay* command is very important for safety as well as good behavior. Dogs must be taught to stay on command until released, especially at doorways, at curbs, and in any other situation in which they may need to be protected. To begin, you'll need to choose a word for the *release* command; it could be "OK." Your dog's attention span will be short at first, so make sure that the first training sessions only involve staying in one place for a few seconds. You'll gradually increase the time he is in stay position as he responds more consistently. Each time you release him from position, use the word "OK" and then reward and praise him for his correct responses.

How to Teach the Stay Command

Start the training session by sitting next to your Cavalier. First, give him the *sit* command. Once he is sitting, give him the *stay* command. Move a short distance from him, continually using the *stay* command. If he moves or gets up, you must begin again. As

During training, you can motivate your Cavalier to learn by rewarding him with a treat and praise when he obeys a command.

soon as he consistently stays, gradually move farther away from him, with you remaining seated. Next, use the *stay* command from a standing position and gradually move farther from him. When he obeys, praise and reward him.

After he has learned that the word "stay" means that he is to sit first and then stay, move the training session to a doorway leading out of the house. Open the door and go out the door while insisting that your dog remain seated. When you are out of the door, use the *release* command and allow your dog to follow you. Repeat this behavior until your dog allows you to stand outside and walk off until you use the *release* command.

Down

Dogs should be taught to stay down. Aside from showing good manners by staying away from dining areas or behaving when visiting the homes of others who may not be dog friendly, it is necessary to keep your dog out of harm's way.

How to Teach the Down *Command*

With training collar and leash attached, put your Cavalier in the sit position. Hold the leash in your left hand and a treat in your right. Rest one hand lightly on top of his shoulders. Do not push down on his back; just let your hand rest there to guide him close to your side when he lies down. Move your right hand in front of his nose and give the *down* command by saying "Down" very quietly, slowly lowering the treat to his front feet. When your hand reaches the floor, keep it moving forward along the floor in front of your dog. He will try to follow the food by lowering himself to the floor. Talk softly to him all the while to reassure him.

When your Cavalier's reaches belly the floor, give him the treat and praise. Try to keep him in the down position for a few seconds while you continue to reassure him. If you pull the treat away too far and too fast, he'll stand up instead of staying down. If you push your hand down on his body and speak sternly, he'll feel threatened and unwilling to obey. Be patient. When he's comfortable with the command, try using your right hand for a signal instead of a treat. Eventually, he will know that the downward hand movement, coupled with the verbal command, means get down.

Once problem behaviors are identified, they can usually be controlled.

Come (Recall)

Aside from the many obvious conveniences, all dogs need to be taught to come to their owner when they are called, no matter what is going on around them, for their own safety. Cavaliers are quite famous for mindlessly chasing a butterfly or ball into oncoming traffic, and knowing the *come* command can save his life.

How to Teach the Come Command

Your Cavalier will need to learn to come on command indoors as well as outdoors, so begin training sessions in the house; this also provides you with a safe and controlled environment. You will need to attach a very long leash to his collar.

To start, give your dog the *stay* command. Next, walk away from him while holding the leash. When you have reached the end of the leash, stop and use the *come* command. On this command, you will also use his call name "Fluffy, come." Now reel the leash in toward you using an encouraging tone of voice the entire time. As soon as your dog reaches you, praise and reward him.

Repeat this indoors until your dog gets the idea, and then move training sessions outdoors. Once he appears to really understand what you are asking him to do, increase the length of the leash and continue to practice on walks and in parks. Always remember to praise him, hug him, and give him small treats. This is one of the most important commands you will ever teach your Cavalier, and no amount of practice is too much.

PROBLEM BEHAVIORS

As you live day to day with your Cavalier, you may notice that he occasionally displays problem behaviors. Sometimes it will be a random behavior, easily corrected by removing the object of his attention, but sometimes dogs develop habits that are annoying and destructive, even dangerous. These behaviors must be addressed, and the correct behavior must be taught and positively reinforced. The most common problem behaviors include aggression, either toward people or other dogs, barking, digging, and chewing.

Aggression

Cavaliers are not usually known to be aggressive dogs; the huge majority of them are not. Your problem with aggression is not likely to be caused by your own dog but because other breeds that may come into contact with him may make him fearful. It is important to recognize what aggression really is, and in the case of your puppy, what it isn't.

When Cavalier puppies are just beginning to toddle about in their pens with their littermates, the first sound that you likely hear coming from there is a humming that sounds a lot like a little beehive. The next sound you hear is the squeal of an unhappy puppy. A quick assessment of the situation invariably yields the same results: One puppy has grabbed another by the ear or the tail and is busily dragging him around the puppy pen. Of course the puppy being dragged about is crying like mad. Mom meanwhile is calmly watching her babies at play. Cavalier puppies play very roughly. They growl at each other as soon as they find their voices, and they gum littermates' ears and tails incessantly. Once they get their little sharp baby teeth, they quickly learn how to use them to their advantage. This is puppy play; it is not aggression, and it is not abnormal behavior.

By the time the puppies are old enough to go to their new homes, they have learned how to play hard and sleep hard. Do not be alarmed if your new puppy drags his toys around by a stuffed ear or tail growling and barking the entire time. This is not aggression. It is play. This is how puppies play. They don't have as large a language as humans do, so the range with which to express themselves is limited. Growling probably means a variety of things to playing puppies, but it isn't a sign of aggression.

Territorial Aggression

Eventually, a puppy begins to learn the meaning of ownership.

Ownership can cause some inappropriate behaviors, especially in youngsters, but these can quickly be controlled with patience and training.

Puppies often get just a little bit "big for their britches" and decide that they own their toys, their owners, and the house and all of its furnishings. This is his territory, and everything in it belongs to him. If another puppy comes to visit, the puppy who "owns" everything in sight will often pounce on the visitor, put him down on his back, and growl at him.

As out of character as it may seem, this isn't unusual for a little Cavalier puppy that is being a bit sassy. It isn't aggression in its true form, and it is relatively easy to control. Simply pick up the visitor and a toy and play with the visitor for a while. Soon, your sassy puppy will want to join in the play, and you can then play with both puppies and verbally reward your puppy for sharing by saying "Good share." Puppies learn very quickly that their naughtiness does not please their owners, and this stage usually passes quickly. Again, this is not aggression; it is simply a learning experience that a bossy little puppy needs to have. Territorial aggression is one of the easiest to manage. The earlier a puppy is exposed to new people, new dogs, and new places, the more quickly he leaves behind territorial aggression. Enrolling your dog in puppy kindergarten is a wonderful activity that can socialize him, teach him good manners, and help him to avoid developing territorial behaviors.

Food Aggression

Begin training your puppy not to be defensive about his food and toys as soon as you bring him home. When he is playing with

Body Language

Our dogs can't sit down and have a heart-to-heart conversation with us to tell us what is troubling them. They communicate with us through their body language. A tail wagging furiously is the universally accepted language for "I'm happy!" But your dog communicates his emotions to you using other gestures and sounds as well. A fearful dog will drop his ears and tail, crouch near his owner, and look toward the ground. An aggressive dog will raise his ears, lift his tail, stop wagging, and exhibit constant eye contact. He will strain at the end of his leash when he is feeling aggressive or anxious.

Studying canine body language can open a window of emotions so that you can observe the state of mind your dog and others may be in and know how to react accordingly.

his toys and chews, reach over frequently and take them out of his mouth. Replace the toy with a different toy. If he reacts by growling, immediately say "No growl" in a firm voice and then stop playing with him. In a few minutes, repeat the action of taking his toy or chew out of his mouth and immediately offering him a new one. When he does not react at all, reward him by saying "Good dog," followed by petting and more verbal praise.

Your puppy wants to please you. He simply needs to know, by the pleasant and calm tone of your voice, what it takes to please you. Eventually, he will associate the words you say with specific behaviors. He will learn that good things happen to him when he lets someone else take his food dish or toy away. Remember that at this point in his life he does not only have to learn which behaviors please you, but he also has to learn human language and which word sounds are associated with each behavior.

Constantly reinforce his good behavior by removing things from his mouth until he has no reaction. Replace the object you have taken with either a small food treat or a favorite toy or chew. Again, this is not so much aggressive behavior as it is instinctual behavior, which will be stronger in some dogs than in others. Careful training and patience from the time the puppy is very young can prevent it.

Aggression With People and Other Dogs

Aggression can be fear-based or the result of protective behavior. When your dog is afraid, his defense mechanism for fear becomes aggression. Protective aggression revolves around protecting his territory and pack, which is now his owner or owners. All responses are inappropriate and must be discouraged if you are to live happily with your Cavalier.

Canine aggression is usually marked by specific body language. It is demonstrated by the lifting of the lips to show the teeth, stiffening of the body, raised hackles, and direct eye contact. The dog's tail will not be wagging. He may be growling, or he may be silent. If your puppy shows you his teeth, stands stiffly with his tail held downward, and stares at you, he is demonstrating aggression toward you.

Some cities in the United States have passed laws requiring that any dog who bites a human must be euthanized. Certainly humans have been traumatized, both physically and emotionally, by dog bites. If your dog has exhibited truly aggressive behaviors

If your dog continually exhibits aggressive behaviors toward you, other people, or other animals, you may need professional help to find solutions.

toward you, other people, or other animals, you will need professional help to find solutions. Do not waste time or think that aggression is a passing phase. On the contrary, the longer this behavior is allowed to continue, the worse it will become. Ask your vet for a referral to an animal behaviorist or contact the American Veterinary Society of Animal Behavior at www. avma.org/avsab for a referral.

An animal behaviorist will teach you how to diffuse your dog's aggressive behavior by using various techniques such as withholding playtime and attention until your dog performs calm behaviors, such as sitting or lying down. This training will also establish you as the leader of the pack and owner of the territory. You may be encouraged to demonstrate that you are the pack leader by refusing to allow him to sleep on the furniture or the bed. You may be taught behavior modification using training tools such as head collars. You will undoubtedly be encouraged to take your dog to obedience training; obedience training is another way to demonstrate to your dog that you are the pack leader and that you are in charge. When dealing with an aggressive dog, it is essential that he learn to be submissive to his owner.

If you are out with your Cavalier and another dog demonstrates or exhibits any of the aggressive behaviors described—lifting of the upper lift to show the teeth, staring, raised hackles, stiff posture, with or without growling—pick up your puppy immediately, and do not maintain eye contact with the dog. Get both you and your dog out of the area as quickly as possible.

It is unlikely that you will experience aggressive behaviors in your Cavalier King Charles Spaniel. Even though it occurs infrequently, it is necessary to be able to recognize inappropriate behaviors sooner rather than later. And it is certainly beneficial to recognize aggression in other dogs, particularly those who approach your Cavalier. Remember that a Cavalier doesn't interpret aggressive signs and signals in the same way most other dogs will in most cases. Their natural instinct is to approach other dogs as potential play friends. It is up to you to read the body language of unfamiliar dogs in order to protect your Cavalier at all times.

Barking

All dogs will bark from time to time; it is a natural canine behavior. It is their method of communicating with you and with other dogs. Barking is how your dog tells you he is excited or hungry, or that he needs to have his water dish filled. Do not expect any dog to be totally silent throughout the day. There are times, however, when barking becomes an annoying habit, and if that happens, you must investigate why he is barking too much and find ways to eliminate this behavior.

First, check your own actions to make certain that it isn't your own overly excited behavior that triggers his barking. Dogs will also often bark for attention if they are left alone for too long, or if they are scared or upset. Never punish your dog for barking. Only when it is habitual, excessive, and inexplicable should you take steps to correct it.

When training your dog not to bark, use the command "No bark." When he has stopped, praise and reward him. Repeat this often. If he has developed barking behaviors during certain predictable activities, try crating him while those activities are occurring. For example, some dogs bark when it is thundering or when lightening is flashing in the room. Crate your dog if you know these weather events are looming. If watching small children running and playing triggers the barking behavior, keep your dog away from those activities.

Any time you are with your dog and he begins to bark excessively, give the command "No bark" and praise and reward him when he stops. This will take lots of repetition and patience, but your dog will eventually learn that excessive barking does not please you. If the barking persists, discuss it with your vet and ask for a referral to an animal behaviorist.

Chewing

Cavalier King Charles Spaniels are not usually destructive

chewers. However, it is certainly understandable that this habit is very distressing to the owners of ruined furniture and personal possessions. Dogs who engage in a lot of destructive chewing are not very picky about their chewing objects either. They will chew shoes, corners of walls, baseboards, furniture of all kinds—just about anything. A leather sofa can be viewed by your little Cavalier as one giant rawhide and pretty much trashed in an afternoon. If restricted to one room, some dogs will try to chew their way out by working on the door or even the walls. Besides the damage, you will want to prevent your dog from getting into something that may be harmful or toxic to him.

Chewing Instinct

Before you can begin to solve chewing problems, you need to understand the reasons behind them. To begin with, dogs are naturally inclined to chew objects. To a dog, chewing is much more than just a behavior, it's a need. Puppies need to chew in order to help them teethe and to grow and exercise their jaws and the muscles that surround the jaws. By 6 weeks of age, your puppy will have his full set of baby teeth. Just as in human babies, these teeth are designed to fall out and be replaced by adult teeth. By 1 year

Finding a Behaviorist

If you feel that you need to employ the services of an animal behaviorist, discuss the issue with your veterinarian. She can most likely recommend a trained professional who will work with you to find solutions to frustrating situations you are unable to deal with on your own. Behaviorists are experts in animal behavior and motivation and will be able to give you advice on how to best solve your pet's problem.

Make an appointment to talk with the behaviorist and explain your dog's behavior issues, the symptoms, and any methods that you've used to try to solve the problem on your own. Ask about her experience in treating your dog's problem. Be sure to get references, find out how many treatment sessions your dog may need, and ask what follow-up training (if any) you will have to do on your own at home. Many behaviorists make house calls and may want to observe your dog in his natural surroundings to better understand the unwanted behavior.

If you can't find a behaviorist locally, check out the websites for the Animal Behavior Society (www.animalbehavior.org), American Veterinary Society of Animal Behavior (www.avma.org/avsab), and International Association of Animal Behavior Consultants (www.iaabc.org).

of age, you can expect your puppy to stop teething and have all of his adult teeth. Of course during teething, your puppy will do a lot of chewing because he will experience some degree of discomfort and pain as his new teeth erupt through the gums. Chewing when his gums hurt is natural and normal; he is only reacting to the pain he feels. He isn't chewing to irritate you or be naughty. When he is feeling the ache of teething, offer him a chew toy that has been placed in the freezer; the cold will feel good to him.

Unfortunately, chewing doesn't end when teething ends. Dogs continue to chew until they are very old and almost toothless. Chewing is fun for a dog—it is recreational. It is enjoyable, soothing, and helps him pass the time. Who can't relate to the fun of ripping up a sofa cushion and sending chunks of the stuffing sailing through the air? However, in the same way that humans often chew their fingernails when they are stressed and unhappy, dogs will chew just about anything they can find if they are feeling nervous or unhappy. If left alone, dogs will often experience separation anxiety, and their need to chew is increased. When their stress is increased, their need to chew is increased. It's just that simple.

Many dog owners mistakenly feel that their pet has ruined a belonging because he is feeling anger toward them. If you come home and find one of your favorite shoes nicely redesigned by your dog's teeth, you may feel that he has purposely punished you for leaving him alone. Actually, nothing could be further from the truth. Dogs don't think in those terms; they don't willfully punish or reward us. They think only in terms of loving us, missing us, wishing they were with us, and being unhappy because we are gone. In fact, when your dog was chewing thoughtfully on your shoe, he was thinking about you. The shoe smells like you. He loves that smell. He can get closer to that smell and closer to you when he chews your shoe than when he sits far away from the shoe admiring it.

As we discussed earlier in the book, chewing can also be a dangerous activity for your dog. Electrical cords can shock or even kill your dog. Even if your Cavalier survives his electrical cord endeavor, he may well be left with serious burns. Dogs who chew and swallow dangerous objects, or objects that are too large to pass, are at risk of bowel obstruction, surgery, or death. Chewing through garbage bags can literally be life threatening if your dog

eats cooked bones, leftover chocolate, or too much paper. It is well worth the time and effort to understand chewing as a behavior and learn how to redirect the behavior to safe chew toys.

How to Redirect Inappropriate Chewing

Now that you understand what chewing is, you are ready to address problem chewing and learn how to direct it toward your dog's toys instead of your belongings. Chewing his own toys is a positive behavior, and with patience and training, you can teach your dog the art of appropriate chewing.

If you have purchased a Cavalier puppy, you will need to start teaching him good habits from the day you bring him home. Coming to an unfamiliar environment opens up a whole new world of chewing delights. As your puppy explores, he will be taking mental notes on all the things that await that special brand of attention only he and his teeth can give. This is the time when you must begin gently redirecting his attention from inappropriate objects to appropriate chew toys. Don't give him old socks or shoes—he can't tell the difference between old shoes and new ones. It is better to make sure that his belongings are his alone and have never belonged to you.

If you come home to find a sofa cushion in pieces and bits of stuffing clinging to your puppy's nose, you have missed your training opportunity. At this point, it's better to crate your puppy for a brief amount of time with a toy or chew and clean up the mess without addressing it. He will not be able to associate your anger with the fun he had an hour ago. Attempt training only when you catch your puppy in the act of chewing on the wrong thing.

Remember that smell is the first thing that will attract a puppy to an object. Unlike humans, dogs enjoy strong, ripe smells. They are very "earthy" creatures and are not offended by odors that repel humans. They especially love your smelly clothes, the enchanting fragrance of garbage cans, and even diapers and cat litter boxes provide a thrill. Go through the house with a fine-toothed comb and remove any of these items from your puppy's reach. Purchase a baby gate or two to cordon off areas that you do not wish your puppy to enter. These gates can often be found in good condition at thrift shops. Make sure that the slats on the gate are close enough together to keep your puppy contained.

If your puppy appears to be entertained by chewing on walls or furniture with hard surfaces, purchase a bitter apple spray product, which is available at pet stores. As a last resort, you can try hot sauce. These solutions may or may not work, depending on how intent your puppy is on chewing, but they are certainly worth a try.

Buying Chew Toys

Cavaliers like having a variety of toys. They enjoy small, stuffed animals and often become bonded to them in much the same way that human babies become bonded to their "blankies" or pacifiers. They often prefer the kinds of soft, stuffed toys made for human babies. Examine each toy carefully for safety prior to purchasing it. Buy a variety of stuffed toys, and keep them in a basket or toy box that is easily accessible to your puppy.

Cavaliers will also need at least six or seven varieties of harder chew toys. Hard nylon bones such as Nylabones and firm rubber

Providing your dog with outlets for his energy may help prevent him from behaving inappropriately.

toys with small holes are especially entertaining. Some of the rubber toys are designed to be filled with small pieces of kibble that come out of them as the puppy rolls them around on the floor. These are especially entertaining because they combine playing, chewing, and eating—always a home run with a Cavalier! It's fun to watch your little puppy carefully going through his toy box searching for his favorites.

Reinforcing Appropriate Chewing

When you see your puppy chewing his own chew toy, praise him enthusiastically. A clicker is also useful for this type of training, just as it was useful for reinforcing his positive behavior when you taught him how to ring a bell to go outdoors. When your puppy is playing or interacting with his own toys, click the clicker and say "Good chew." Use a positive, fun tone of voice. The clicker can assist you with positive reinforcement.

Another popular method of discouraging your dog from inappropriate behavior is to use a noise-making device, such as an empty can with a few pennies placed inside. Tape the can securely

To dogs, digging is an instinctive behavior.

closed after you have placed the coins inside. If the dog is chewing something that he should not be chewing, shake the can to startle him with the noise. Never throw the can at the puppy. Just shake it near him and say "No" in a firm voice. Then, quickly give him one of his own toys and say "Good chew" in a positive, encouraging manner. At this time, it helps to play with the puppy and his toy to reinforce his correct response.

Again, safety is the primary concern with chewers, especially those who chew out of separation anxiety. Consult your vet about options for dealing with this issue, but meanwhile, protect your Cavalier from chewing something potentially dangerous by crating him while you're out. If he's properly crate trained, this shouldn't be a problem. If he's still in the process of crate training and hasn't yet learned to like being left in it, grit your teeth and crate him anyway. His safety must take precedence over his temporary unhappiness during your brief absence.

Digging

You may find that your little Cavalier never digs at all. But one day, your friend drops by for a visit bringing along her new terrier puppy. You both decide that the two puppies might have fun together playing in the back yard while you visit with each other. Then, to your great surprise, you discover that your Cavalier has learned an entirely new behavior. When you go outdoors to retrieve the puppies, you find them both covered in dirt from head to toe, and you may be even more surprised to discover that you now possess a number of new holes in which to plant flowers.

Dogs dig for a variety of reasons. They are denning animals by nature, and their ancestors dug holes in which they lived and whelped their litters. They also dug to hunt for food. Your dog may dig to escape your yard in search of one thing or another, but for his safety, he must be taught not to dig at all. If your puppy digs his way out of the yard, he is at risk of being stolen, hit by a car, or attacked by another dog. It's best to try to head off this particular problem right from the start.

If your puppy or adult dog is left alone in the yard for long periods of time, especially if he has been left without toys or other means of entertaining himself, he may turn to digging as entertainment. Digging is fun, and dogs are well equipped for it with their strong upper arms and sharp nails. Besides, dirt smells

Adding Another Dog

If your Cavalier has been experiencing problem behaviors, you might consider adding a second dog to the family. By nature, all canines are pack animals; they are used to living in groups. Perhaps your dog has misbehaved simply because he is forced to spend too much time alone. All dogs enjoy the companionship of other dogs, and Cavaliers are no exception.

When your current dog is well on the way to being secure in housetraining and general household behavior, you can add a second one to your family. If you are unable to bring in another dog to act as a companion, consider setting aside specific days and times for play dates with other dogs, or take your Cavalier to the dog park or to doggy day care if you are away from home often.

Most of all, your dog wants to be with you. Whether it is during active playtime, exercise, or just sitting on the couch cuddling and watching TV, he wants to spend as much time with you as you can offer. A second dog would be like frosting on the cake because your Cavalier's life revolves around you most of all.

interesting and digging offers earthworms and small bugs that mean long minutes of entertainment prior to being gobbled up by the lucky finder.

If your Cavalier has not been given enough exercise or play time, he may well turn to digging as a substitute. To prevent the problem, exercise your puppy frequently and play with him often during the day. If you are physically unable to do this, you can still offer several exercises that don't involve a lot of walking. For example, sit in a chair in your house or back yard and throw a ball for a good game of fetch. Tug toys are great exercise but often don't require a great deal of physical mobility on your part.

If your dog persists in pursuing his subterranean activities, teach him the command "No dig." Each time you catch him in the act of digging, approach him with one of his toys, say "No dig," and give him the toy. As soon as he takes the toy in his mouth, say "Good toy" and praise him enthusiastically, letting your tone of voice be his best reward.

You will find that your dog does not enjoy long periods of time in the yard unless you are there with him. Most Cavaliers do not dig at all, but if yours resorts to digging as a pastime, work hard to educate him that digging is unacceptable behavior or you could run the risk of losing him to an accident of some sort.

Separation Anxiety

Some dogs suffer considerably from separation anxiety. They do not know where you have gone, when you are returning, or why they were left behind. When you return, they are wildly out of control but appear to be exceedingly happy to see you. As with other behavior problems, it's always best to prevent this problem by addressing it when your Cavalier is a puppy. As with humans, leaving your mom and littermates and going to a new home can be very stressful for a pet.

The best way to avoid separation anxiety is to crate your puppy in your absence unless you are going to be gone for more than two to three hours. If you are going to be gone for a longer period of

To prevent separation anxiety, make sure your dog has a variety of toys to play with when he is alone.

Training will help your Cavalier become a well-behaved member of your family.

time, place the crate within a fenced or small gated area and leave the door to the crate open so that your puppy can retreat to it when he wants. Provide him with water and several toys and chews. Do not let him watch you putting on your coat, finding your car keys, and preparing to go. Do not make a point of telling him goodbye. In fact, if you can leave without drawing any attention to your leaving at all, this is desirable.

When you come back, don't draw attention to yourself or your arrival. Take the time to hang up your coat and put away your things and then very calmly go into the room where your puppy has been confined. Remove him from his crate quietly and calmly, and take him to the designated potty area. After your puppy has relieved himself, spend some quiet time with him. Talk to him in a quiet soothing tone of voice and then play with him more enthusiastically.

If you draw a lot of attention to yourself as you are leaving, and if you allow your puppy to jump wildly on you barking frantically, you are reinforcing his anxieties. By giving him the idea that leaving is an act worthy of his attention and that returning is an act worthy of his frantic behaviors, you have reinforced his separation anxiety. After he has passed through the puppy stage and can safely be allowed to remain unconfined in the house, he will replace those frantic greetings by having been taught to have a toy in his mouth for some play time when you arrive home. Be sure that when your dog is alone, you have provided him with a variety of interesting toys. Leaving a radio on is often very soothing to a puppy alone in the house.

BE PATIENT AND POSITIVE

When it comes to working with puppies and dogs, positive reinforcement works much more effectively than negative reinforcement or punishment. Dogs will not understand the concept of punishment because they don't understand the concept of being "naughty." Remember, your Cavalier puppy wants to please you—that truly is his goal and his desire. By learning ways to let him know that he has pleased you and that he has done the right thing, you will be able to positively reinforce his good behaviors while at the same time discouraging his negative behaviors.

ADVANCED TRAINING *and* ACTIVITIES

With Your Cavalier King Charles Spaniel

Your Cavalier will enjoy any activity as long as he gets to do it with you. He will enjoy everything from basic obedience to agility. Cavaliers do particularly well in agility, but as you may guess, they thrive as therapy dogs. If you find, as many people do, that you enjoy the time you spend training your dog and being with other people who love dogs, you might want to try some of these more advanced activities. Whether you participate in dog sports just for fun, to earn titles, or to strive for high-level awards and honors, the time you spend will enhance the bond you share with your dog. So, get involved with your dog! The exercise is good for both of you.

CANINE GOOD CITIZEN® TEST

Starting in 1989, the American Kennel Club (AKC) began sponsoring the Canine Good Citizen (CGC) program. It is one of the fastest growing of all the AKC programs. The CGC program has two parts: The first part stresses responsible pet ownership by encouraging owners to foster and encourage good manners in their dogs, and the second part rewards dogs who are able to demonstrate exceptional manners and socialization skills. This work will lay a foundation for future obedience and agility work. All dogs who pass the 10-step program will receive a certificate from the AKC.

As you and your dog work together to win the CGC certificate, you will begin to tap into the immeasurable pleasures that can be found working with an animal. Continually training and teaching your dog encourages and builds the bond you share. What's more, dogs who have been well trained and socialized are a joy to be with and are good ambassadors for their breed and dogs in general.

Since the AKC began this program, many other countries such as England, Japan, and Australia have developed similar programs based on it. Therapy groups have used the CGC program as a screening tool, and 4-H groups have used it as a beginner's program to teach children how to train their dogs. Several specialty clubs give the CGC certificate at their national shows. Veterinarians have recognized the value of the program and have advocated it as a tool toward responsible dog ownership as well. In just over 10 years, this important program has had an extremely positive influence on how dogs are perceived by nonowners. It helps to assure that our dogs will be welcome and well-respected members of our communities.

Before taking the CGC test, dog owners are asked to sign the Responsible Dog Owner's Pledge. By signing that pledge, they agree to take care of their dog's health needs, exercise, training, quality of life, and safety. They are also taking full responsibility for cleaning up after their dogs in public places. Both owners and their dogs are encouraged to respect the rights of others.

The test consists of 10 parts as follows:

Test 1: Accepting a Friendly Stranger

This test demonstrates that the dog will allow a friendly stranger to approach him and speak to his handler. The evaluator will walk up to the dog and handler and greet the handler in a friendly manner, ignoring the dog. The evaluator and handler will then shake hands and exchange pleasantries. The dog must show no signs of resentment or shyness, and must not break position or try to go to the evaluator.

Whatever your reasons for continuing to train, working regularly with your Cavalier will strengthen the bond between you, direct his energy in a positive way, and help keep him fit and trim.

Test 2: Sitting Politely for Petting

This test demonstrates that the dog will allow a friendly stranger to touch him while he is out and about with his handler. With the dog sitting at the handler's side, the evaluator will pet the dog on the head and body. The handler may talk to her dog throughout the exercise. The dog may stand in place as he is petted but must not show shyness or resentment.

Test 3: Appearance and Grooming

This practical test demonstrates that the dog will welcome being groomed and examined, and will permit someone such as a veterinarian, groomer, or friend of the owner to do so. It also demonstrates the owner's care, concern, and sense of responsibility. The evaluator will inspect the dog to determine if he is clean and groomed. The dog must appear to be in healthy condition (i.e., proper weight, clean, healthy, and alert). The handler should supply the comb or brush commonly used on the dog. The evaluator will then softly comb or brush the dog, and in a natural manner, lightly examine the ears and gently pick up each front foot. It is not necessary for the dog to hold a specific position during the examination, and the handler may talk to the dog, praise him, and give encouragement throughout.

Test 4: Out for a Walk (Walking on a Loose Lead)

This test demonstrates that the handler is in control of the dog. The dog may be on either side of the handler. The dog's position should leave no doubt that he is attentive to the handler and is responding to the handler's movements and changes of direction. The dog need not be perfectly aligned with the handler, and need not sit when the handler stops. The evaluator may use a preplotted course or may direct the handler/dog team by issuing instructions or commands. In either case, there should be a right turn, left turn, and an about turn with at least one stop in between and another at the end. The handler may talk to the dog along the way, praise the dog, or give commands in a normal tone of voice. The handler may sit the dog at the halts if desired.

Test 5: Walking Through a Crowd

This test demonstrates that the dog can move about politely in pedestrian traffic and is under control in public places. The dog and handler will walk around and pass close to several people (at least three). The dog may show some interest in the strangers but should continue to walk with the handler, without evidence of over-exuberance, shyness, or resentment. The handler may talk to the dog and encourage or praise the dog throughout the test. The dog should not jump on people in the crowd or strain on the leash.

Test 6: Sit and Down on Command and Staying in Place

This test demonstrates that the dog has training, will respond

The Canine Good Citizen test encourages owners to foster and encourage good manners in their dogs.

to the handler's commands to sit and down, and will remain in the place when commanded by the handler (sit or down position, whichever the handler prefers). The dog must do sit and down on command; the owner chooses the position for leaving the dog in the stay. Prior to this test, the dog's leash is replaced with a line 20 feet (6 m) long. The handler may take a reasonable amount of time and use more than one command to get the dog to sit and then down. The evaluator must determine if the dog has responded to the handler's commands. The handler may not force the dog into position but may touch the dog to offer gentle guidance. When instructed by the evaluator, the handler will tell the dog to stay and walk forward the length of the line, turn, and return to the dog at a natural pace. The dog must remain in the place in which he was left (he may change position) until the evaluator instructs the handler to release the dog. The dog may be released from the front or the side.

Test 7: Coming When Called

This test demonstrates that the dog will come when called by the handler. The handler will walk 10 feet (3 m) from the dog, turn to face the dog, and call the dog. The handler may use encouragement to get the dog to come. Handlers may choose to tell dogs to "stay" or "wait," or they may simply walk away, giving no instructions to the dog.

Test 8: Reaction to Another Dog

This test demonstrates that the dog can behave politely around other dogs. Two handlers and their dogs will approach each other from a distance of about 20 feet (6 m), stop, shake hands, exchange pleasantries, and continue on for about 10 feet (3 m). The dogs should show no more than casual interest in each other. Neither dog should go to the other dog or his handler.

Test 9: Reaction to Distraction

This test demonstrates that the dog is confident at all times when faced with common distracting situations. The evaluator will select and present two distractions. Examples of distractions include dropping a chair, rolling a crate dolly past the dog, having a jogger run in front of the dog, or dropping a crutch or cane. The dog may express natural interest and curiosity and/or may appear slightly startled but should not panic, try to run away, show aggressiveness, or bark. The handler may talk to the dog and encourage or praise him throughout the exercise.

Test 10: Supervised Separation

This test demonstrates that a dog can be left with a trusted person, if necessary, and will maintain training and good manners. Evaluators are encouraged to say something like, "Would you like me to watch your dog?" and then take hold of the dog's leash. The owner will go out of sight for three minutes. The dog does not have to stay in position but should not continually bark, whine, or pace unnecessarily, or show anything stronger than mild agitation or nervousness. Evaluators may talk to the dog but should not engage in excessive talking, petting, or attempts to manage him (e.g., "there, there, it's alright").

Being Prepared for the CGC Test

Before taking the CGC test, you will need to have a few pieces of equipment. Your dog will need a buckle or slip collar, leash, and brush; the evaluator supplies the 20-foot (6-m) lead for the test.

Food and treats are not permitted during testing, nor is the use of toys. Any dog who eliminates during the test will be dismissed except possibly during Test 10, provided that Test 10 takes place in an outdoor setting. Any dog who growls, snaps, bites, attacks, or attempts to attack a person or another dog is not a candidate for the CGC award and will dismissed from the test.

THERAPY WORK

Once your dog is well socialized, you may share the joy of your Cavalier with someone who would not ordinarily be able to spend time with a pet. In recent years, mounting evidence has suggested that pets are a tonic to human health, lowering stress, reducing blood pressure levels, and adding to our general sense of well-being. Consequently, there has been a rise in the number of animals visiting patients in hospitals and nursing homes. Cavaliers make exceptionally good therapy dogs because of their sunny temperament, friendly little personalities, and willingness to snuggle and cuddle with everyone. They are small enough to sit on a lap and sweet enough to enjoy loving attention from everyone. They really are the ideal little therapy dogs.

Cavaliers who are being considered for therapy work must be trained and tested. The training is probably the easiest part of all because being loving, sweet, and cuddly is an innate part of their temperaments. Those skills are not new behaviors for Cavaliers! Testing ensures dogs are suited for therapy work and safe around people in unusual settings: people using walkers, in beds and wheelchairs, and in busy institutional environments. It involves determining that the dog is polite and easily controlled by his handler. The handler–dog team will need to demonstrate their ability to walk together with the dog on a loose lead going forward, turning, and stopping. The dog is expected to be able to approach people who are unsteady on their feet or immobile. He must not show fear of the people he is meeting, but instead be quiet and well-behaved, exhibiting pleasure upon meeting friendly strangers. He should comfortably accept handling, stroking, petting, and touching of the paws and ears. If other dogs are present during the therapy sessions, he is expected to ignore them and focus on the therapy patient. The tester will want to see that the Cavalier appears to be willing to be a therapy dog and accepting of the exercises. He is expected to respond to therapy work in a happy

and calmly accepting way. The team will be judged on appearance as well. Both Cavalier and handler are expected to be well-groomed and clean. Cavaliers make wonderful therapy dogs, and the time spent working with patients is very rewarding.

OUTDOOR ACTIVITIES AND SPORTS

Lots of people and their dogs have discovered the joy of attending advanced classes just for fun or to prepare for competition. Whatever your reasons for continuing to train, working regularly with your Cavalier will strengthen the bond between you, direct your Cavalier's energy in a positive way, and help keep him fit and trim. Let's look at some of the activities you might enjoy together.

Walking With Your Cavalier

Cavaliers love going for walks. Extremely social animals, they thrive on both the activity and the opportunity to "meet and greet" neighbors, other dogs, and anyone who stops simply to admire them. A Cavalier can spot another Cavalier from a mile away, and make no mistake about it, they know that they have something in common. Cavaliers are quite well-known for preferring to be with other Cavaliers of their own color, but on a walk around the neighborhood, any other Cavalier will do. Walking provides a good opportunity for your dog to learn acceptable behavior during these encounters.

Daily walks are a necessary and beneficial part of dog ownership. Taking your adult Cavalier for a brisk walk will benefit his health as well as yours. Dogs who get into mischief at home are often bored, and the best way to prevent boredom is with activity. Walking and jogging are also good ways to keep your Cavalier's toenails naturally trimmed. In fact, a sign that your dog isn't getting enough exercise is if his toenails grow too long. Paved surfaces are nature's nail trimmers.

Be mindful of weather conditions when journeying outdoors. On very hot days, it's best to stay cool indoors and save the walk for less oppressive temperatures. Likewise, if it's really cold out, keep the walk short and brisk, and perhaps have your dog wear a sweater.

Sports and Outdoor Safety

Whenever you engage in outdoor activities with your dog, take precautions to make sure that he is not subject to dangers in the immediate environment or to extremes in weather.

For example, many plants are toxic to dogs. Teach the command "Leave it" early on and discourage plant chewing. After outdoor training sessions, examine your dog's coat and feet to make sure that he has not picked up thorns or other objects. Also, use good flea and tick protection.

On hot days, make sure your dog does not overheat. Be sure he is hydrated and has cool water to drink. You can spray a light mist of water into his coat and ruffle it through to the skin. Evaporation of the mist will assist in keeping him calm, cool, and collected. Be mindful of weather conditions when training outdoors. On very hot days, it's best to stay cool indoors and save training for less oppressive temperatures.

Fetch

Cavaliers can be taught almost any dog sport that other small breeds of dog can learn. Playing fetch is a simple sport that dog and owner can enjoy equally. Many Cavaliers have a natural instinct to retrieve objects that are thrown for them. Some do not, however, so it is wise to allow your puppy to demonstrate to you what he enjoys doing.

You can start teaching your Cavalier to retrieve by tossing a small stuffed toy a few feet (a meter or two) away. Once he has the toy in his mouth, call him to you by saying "Come." When he has brought the toy back to you, praise him generously and enthusiastically. It only takes a few repetitions for your puppy to learn that retrieval can be fun. As the puppy gets older, you will be able to switch to a ball thrown for longer distances. Even a child can teach a Cavalier to retrieve. Fetch is a great game for children and dogs to enjoy together.

Agility

Agility is a wonderful activity for dogs. It requires a moderate amount of physical activity from both the owner/handler and the dog. Your Cavalier will learn to run, jump over specific objects laid out on a course, and run through tunnels and weave poles. During

In the sport of agility, your Cavalier will learn to jump over objects laid out on a course and run through tunnels and weave poles.

competition, the owner/handler runs alongside the various objects on the course while her dog runs the course in a timed race. It's a lot of fun for the dogs, wonderful bonding time with the owner, and great exercise for everyone. Your local kennel club will have information about locations where agility is taught in your area.

Canine Freestyle

Steadily gaining in popularity, canine freestyle, or "dancing with dogs," is a competitive dog sport that combines obedience and dance to display teamwork and rapport between dog and handler. Routines are set to music of all kinds, and as the handler dances in rhythm to the music, the dog is taught to dance along, jump over the handler, and perform other moves. Sometimes the handlers and dogs wear costumes. It is a great deal of fun to watch, and dogs and handlers alike love the activity. It also makes a great exhibition event at schools, hospitals, and nursing homes.

Rally-O

The dog world owes a bow and a handshake to Mr. Bud Cort, who is credited with coming up with both agility and rally-o. Rally-o is often a very satisfying event for older dogs who haven't previously competed in other competitions because it is less rigid and precise in the rules that govern scoring, and it allows unlimited communication. The handler can talk to her dog and give repeated commands and hand signals. It's similar to obedience, but has a fun little twist.

The dog and handler team move through a rally course of 10 to 20 signs. As in most dog training events, the dog will be expected to be at the left side of the handler. Each sign indicates which behavior is desired from the dog, and the handler is allowed unrestricted communication with the dog to elicit that behavior. The dog can also be given small food treats by the handler when his performance is pleasing, but there is a small penalty if the dog drops his treat. Scoring is less rigorous, but the event is still a competition. The goal of rally-o is fun, fun, fun, and both dogs and handlers truly enjoy this increasingly popular sport.

SHOWING YOUR DOG

The decision to show your dog must be made carefully. A tremendous commitment must be made both in buying a dog for

At a dog show, dogs are judged against the standard for the breed.

showing and in maintaining him in show condition until such time that you decide to retire him from the show ring. A dog for showing must come as close to his breed standard as possible. Dog shows are not beauty contests or obedience competitions. They are not shows to see which dog is the prettiest or which dog has the most perfect markings. A dog show is not designed to pit one dog against another to see which one behaves best in the show ring. Dog shows are actually far more serious than that. They are held to give serious breeders an opportunity to see how the dogs that they are producing measure up against dogs from other kennels. Dog showing is all about structure and the standard of perfection for the breed.

Doing Your Homework

Before contemplating the purchase of a show-quality Cavalier, learn the breed standard and attend a few dog shows. If you visit kennels prior to doing so, you may not choose the right type of dog for showing. Cavalier puppies are so winning and delightful that, before you know it, you will have fallen in love with a puppy and you will want to take him home with you. Resist the temptation until you have done your research. There is no reason to rush this step. You will have your dog for many years, and a few months of research will only make the process of showing your dog more enjoyable.

Attending Shows

Once you have learned the breed standard, attend a few dog shows. It is fairly easy to find out where the shows will be held by looking at the AKC website's listing of AKC-sanctioned dog shows in your area. You can also type "AKC Dog Shows" into your computer's search engine and get a lot of information. Shows are sponsored by different kennel clubs in each regional area. The kennel clubs make arrangements with a "show superintendent" to run the show. He contacts the exhibitors in his area, sending them information about upcoming shows. He then collects the entry fees and entry information and prints a catalogue. These catalogues are available for purchase and can help you to navigate your way around a show.

The classes will be broken into puppy dog and adult dog classes and puppy bitch and adult bitch classes. Dogs are shown first, and bitches are shown immediately following dogs. This order of showing is universal. At larger shows, the puppy classes sometimes include a 12- to 15-month class followed by a 15- to 18-month class, but normal dog shows have the classes listed below. All classes are as follows:

- Puppy Dog 6 to 9 months
- Puppy Dog 9 to 12 months
- Puppy Dog 12 to 18 months
- Novice Dog
- Bred by Exhibitor Dog
- American Bred Dog
- Open Dog
- Winner's Class
- Puppy Bitch 6 to 9 months
- Puppy Bitch 9 to 12 months
- Puppy Bitch 12 to 18 months
- Novice Bitch
- Bred by Exhibitor Bitch
- American Bred Bitch
- Open Bitch
- Winner's Class

Anyone new to dog showing should know that there is never any money to be won at a standard dog show. The wins are points represented by different ribbons. The dogs who win class points are the Winner's Dog and Winner's Bitch. Those points will go toward

AKC Ribbons

An AKC award-winning dog receives a ribbon from the judge that indicates what type of conformation award he has won:

- Blue—first place in any regular class
- Red—second place in each class
- Yellow—third place in each class
- White—fourth place in each class
- Purple—Winner's Dog and Winner's Bitch classes
- Purple and White—Runners-up in Winner's Dog and Winner's Bitch classes
- Blue and White—Best of Winner's (chosen between Winner's Dog and Winner's Bitch)
- Purple and Gold—Best in Breed in each competition
- Red and White—Best of Opposite Sex (to Best in Breed Winner)
- Red, White, and Blue—Best in Show

the 15 points necessary for a championship title. The vast majority of class dogs will end their show career the day they become AKC champions. The dog or bitch who wins Best of Breed receives a point for each dog defeated from the classes.

Finding a Show-Quality Puppy

Most breeders produce more quality puppies in a year than they can keep and are always willing to place one in a beginning show-dog home. Nice bitch puppies are generally at a premium, and a good breeder will want to keep them to be shown and later to be utilized in a breeding program. This is a plain fact of life and a reality of professional breeding; the best of the best will always be kept by the breeder. However, because many breeders only keep one or two dogs at a time, you can often find one who will be willing to work with you and sell you a nice male puppy. After you are well established in the show world, many breeders will trust you enough to place a nice female with you, but if you are new this is not usually the case.

The search for a show dog begins with a search for a breeder. Check breed websites first because they will always have a list.

Here are some basic but important guidelines:

- Do not buy from backyard breeders.
- Do not buy from a newspaper ad.
- Do not buy from the Internet.
- Do not buy from a breeder who takes credit cards.
- Do not buy from a breeder who will not allow you to see at least the dam and pictures of the sire.
- Do not pay too much attention to statements such as

"from championship stock" or "many champions in the pedigree." These aren't really very meaningful statements. If you go back far enough into the pedigrees of any puppy, you will eventually find champions.

Always interview prospective breeders by asking the following questions:

1. Do you health test your breeding animals?

Health testing of the breeding stock is an important part of being a responsible breeder. If a breeder is not health testing, eliminate that breeder from your list immediately. All purebred dogs have health issues of one kind or another.

2. May I see the health test results on the parents and the puppy?

If the answer is no, eliminate that breeder from your list. If a breeder is health testing the breeding animals within the kennel, they should be willing to show the results to you. Even more desirable is that they provide you with copies of health-testing results for the puppy and his or her parents once the purchase is complete.

3. Do you have a health guarantee on your puppies?

Many breeders have some sort of a health guarantee. Ask what the terms of the guarantee are and whether you are to get a copy of the guarantee when the purchase of the puppy is complete.

4. Do you show your dogs?

If you are seeking a show dog, you should be seeking it from a "show breeder." Show breeders have had many opportunities to see how their dogs compare with other dogs being shown. A breeder who also shows will be familiar with the breed standard and more able to assist you in a careful assessment of the puppy.

5. Will the breeder require a "co-own"?

Co-owning a show dog is a common practice. Often a breeder will sell a puppy to you with the understanding that they will

Attending handling classes will prepare you and your Cavalier for the show ring.

continue to be on the registration as a co-owner. Sometimes co-ownership involves lifetime breeding rights, and sometimes it ends at a specified time. If there is to be a co-ownership contract, ask for the specifics up front. When does it end? Does it involve breeding the dog? Are puppies to be returned to the owner breeding their bitch puppy?

Handling Classes

Once you have chosen your puppy, your breeder can direct you to a location that holds handling classes. She can also act as a mentor to you as you begin your dog's show career. Your show catalogues will also list contact information about kennels offering handling classes.

You can work on a few things at home to prepare your puppy for the ring, even when he is too young for handling classes. Once he has learned to exhibit his teeth, walk on your left side on lead, stand and back up on command, and stand on a table, he is ready to go to handling classes. Classes are usually held weekly, and often a nominal fee is charged for each class you attend. After you have attended handling classes, you are ready to begin showing your puppy.

Competition

Judges cannot make every exhibitor happy. As you leave the show ring at the end of the competition, only two of the dogs shown will win class points, and only the Best of Breed (BOB) winner will have BOB points. The job of the judge is to award points to the dog and the bitch who most closely approximate the breed standard; the very best of all the dogs shown will win BOB.

Judges have studied the breed standard carefully in preparation for the show and must meet certain qualifications to earn judging status. They are given a very short amount of time to make the assessments of each dog. They not only look for structure and movement but for a pleasing overall presentation as well: Is the dog well groomed? Does he appear to enjoy what he is doing? Is he generally well mannered? Does he go around the ring easily with the other dogs or is he constantly fighting the lead? At the same time, the judge must be checking toplines, rear ends, shoulder layback, and all of the other characteristics put forth in the breed standard.

When a dog is placed on the judging table, the judge will put his hands on the dog to check body structure, which is felt through the coat. Dogs must have both testicles to compete in the show ring, and bitches must be intact. The judge will open the dog's mouth, or ask you to do so. At this point, you will be grateful for the many practice exercises you did saying "Teeth" to your puppy until he sweetly and willingly showed you his teeth. As a general rule of courtesy, do not try to engage the judge in a conversation at this time. Allow him to assess your dog, and answer any questions he may ask you. Judges will often want to know the age of the dog they are examining. After the show has finished, you may be able to approach the judge, time permitting.

VERSATILITY

The Cavalier's natural warmth and generous nature make him a great candidate for a variety of activities, from therapy work to sports. You'll find that a well-trained, well-socialized dog is not only a pleasure to have with you, but a wonderful role model for his breed.

What to Wear When Showing Your Cavalier

In show rings, both in the United States and Europe, you will see men and women wearing attractive but serviceable business attire. Men usually wear jackets and ties, and women wear pant suits or business-appropriate dresses and skirts. Avoid sandals or strappy shoes that will flop around on your feet. These may distract your dog from the business at hand. Pockets are an absolute must, as are sleeves to which will be affixed your dog's number. Choose clothing that provides a pleasant background for your dog; think of yourself as the artist's canvas against which your dog will be presented. Solid, neutral colors that don't hold or show dog hair are preferable. Heavyweight silks work very well in the show ring because they shed dog hair. Most importantly, don't wear anything that will draw attention away from your Cavalier. After all, he's the real star of the show.

HEALTH

of Your Cavalier King Charles Spaniel

Cavaliers are generally healthy, happy little dogs. They have plenty of the energy and stamina required to keep up with the activities of their families. All purebred dogs have health issues of one kind or another specific to their particular breed; however, regularly scheduled appointments with your vet can alert you to these problems should they arise.

Annual veterinary exams are also necessary to keep your Cavalier's immunizations current and to give him the opportunity to be physically assessed. An attentive owner and regular checkups will help ensure your dog will live a long and healthy life.

THE FIRST LINE OF DEFENSE: HEALTH CHECKS DURING GROOMING

A complete nose-to-tail health check should be a regular part of your grooming procedures. As you groom your Cavalier, you have the perfect opportunity to examine his eyes, ears, skin, and feet for problems. Although other areas can cause health issues, these are the most common. You can easily learn to perform this body check and make it part of your dog's normal grooming routine.

Examining the Eyes

Because Cavaliers have large eyes, they frequently suffer from small injuries to the surface of the eyeball. However, some of these injuries can escalate into more serious conditions. For example, a scratch on the cornea can quickly become infected, leading to ulcerations and eventual blindness if not treated by a vet. Your Cavalier may also suffer from other types of eye disorders or conditions, some genetic and some not. It's always a good idea to know what is normal and what is not so that you can take appropriate action.

Check your dog's eyes carefully during each grooming session. If he appears to be blinking often or favoring one eye, this may indicate he has incurred some sort of injury. Keep him under very close observation for a few hours. During this time, you can use normal saline solution to rinse off the surface of the eye in case a hair or piece of debris is causing the irritation. If there is no sign of improvement within an hour or two, take your dog to the vet. Excessive tearing or abnormal amounts of discharge in the inner corners of the eye can be a sign of infection and will require treatment by your vet.

Corneal Scratches

Injuries to the cornea can occur if your dog runs into a sharp object or during play with another dog. If the eye appears "cloudy," consider it an emergency requiring immediate veterinary attention. Cloudiness that appears suddenly is usually a common indication of an injury to the eye. However, cloudiness developing over a longer period of time that gradually worsens is an indication of other more serious problems, such as dystrophy or cataracts.

The problem with eye injuries is that they can progress so rapidly that there is no time to waste. In some cases, the cornea may ulcerate causing inflammation, pain, and eventual damage. One of the more successful treatments for corneal ulcers is the use of the dog's own blood, spun down to a clear serum and used as an eye drop. Ask your vet about the possibility of using serum to cure the corneal ulcer. Your vet may wish to treat the injury with an antibiotic drop or ointment. If the ulceration appears to be very slow to heal, the use of serum in combination with antibiotic drops should be considered.

Annual veterinary checkups are essential if you want your dog to stay healthy.

Corneal Dystrophy

Corneal dystrophy is a condition that affects the cornea, the transparent front of the eye. It is often the result of an accumulation of cholesterol crystals that deposit on the surface of the cornea. These may appear as grayish white lines, circles, or clouding, causing blurred or unclear vision.

Although corneal dystrophy may not significantly affect

vision in the early stages, it does require proper evaluation and treatment for restoration of optimal vision. Initial treatment may include eye drops and/or ointment to reduce the corneal swelling. Some cases may be corrected surgically.

The different types of corneal dystrophy are divided into subdivisions determined by the location of the dystrophy, and treatment is administered accordingly.

Cataracts

Cataracts are defined as opacity (cloudiness) of the lens of the eye, a condition that causes loss of functional vision. They can occur in one or both eyes and may develop rapidly or take several years to fully develop.

Cataracts can be diagnosed by a canine ophthalmologist well before they can be seen with the naked eye. They are usually considered to be somewhat genetic in nature, but some experts attribute their development to poor nutrition in puppies. Also, just as in humans, some cataracts are strictly age-related and occur in older dogs.

Once a cataract has developed, it is irreversible and may progress to eventual blindness. Artificial lens replacement is available for dogs, but there is no guarantee that it can restore vision adequately.

Distichiasis

Distichiasis is an abnormality of the eye in which the eyelashes grow toward the eye instead of away from the eye. This can cause constant irritation that is mild in nature, resulting in increased tearing, or it can be more serious, resulting in ulceration of the cornea. It is a fairly easy condition to remedy and is commonly corrected with laser surgery.

Dry Eye Syndrome

Dry eye syndrome is a condition in which the eye does not produce enough tears to keep the eye moist and clean. If the eye is only mildly affected, it can be treated with an eye drop designed to moisten the eye and replace the tears. If it is severe, it can lead to ulceration of the eye and blindness, sometimes by an early age. Although easy to diagnose, it can be difficult to treat in the most severe cases.

Entropion

Entropion is considered an inherited condition in most purebred dogs. It is characterized by the rolling in of the eyelid, which causes the eyelashes to rub against the eyeball, causing painful ulcerations or erosion of the cornea.

Entropion can be surgically treated and rarely reoccurs once surgery is performed. Because it is genetic in nature, affected dogs, their parents, and unaffected siblings should not be used for breeding.

Microphthalmia

Microphthalmia is a condition of the eye in which the third eyelid (located in the inner corner of the eye) is very prominent and the eye is small and recessed into the socket. In mild cases, there is usually no visual impairment, but in moderate to severe cases, there is almost certainly some degree of visual impairment, including blindness. Because it is believed to be genetic in nature, affected dogs, their parents, and siblings should not be used for breeding.

Examining the Ears

A foul odor can be an indication of infection or the presence of

Cavaliers tend to suffer more eye injuries than other breeds because they have large eyes.

a foreign body in the ear canal. Smell the ear, then lift the ear flap and examine it closely. Look carefully at the interior, and check for discharge or a crusty substance. Using a dampened white washcloth (white allows you to see the color of any discharge present), gently wipe the ear flap and the outer ear. Because the canine ear canal is shaped somewhat like an "L," you must never attempt to use swabs to clean any part of the interior of the ear, only the visible part at the surface.

Ear Infections

You'll want to perform a routine inspection of your dog's ears. This will enable you to spot any parasites, irritations, or discharge that could indicate a problem. This is easily done during every grooming session.

Your Cavalier's ears should always have a healthy overall appearance and smell. Dark brown or black pasty-looking discharge may be an indication of a yeast infection, a bacterial infection, or both. Medication will be required to treat the problem, so you will need to make an appointment with your vet. She will decide which type of medication to administer after a microscopic examination of the secretions of the ear identifies the specific organism causing the infection. The medication may be antibacterial or anti-yeast and fungus, or a combination of the two.

Ear Mites

If your Cavalier has been scratching at his ears a lot, it may be an indication that he has parasites such as ear mites or a skin mite called *Cheyletiella*, also known as "walking dandruff" or "rabbit mites." *Cheyletiella* is highly contagious, so if you have more than one dog, you will probably need to treat them all. Also be especially watchful of excessive matting on the fur around the ears during your regular examinations because this is often the result of constantly "scratching the itch" caused by the mites.

Examining the Mouth and Teeth

As a part of the grooming process, always examine your dog's mouth, gums, and teeth. Canine teeth will often develop tartar over time. Also examine the gums. If they are reddened and swollen, your dog is probably suffering from gum disease, which must be treated by your vet. Tooth and gum infections are often implicated in heart disease and other problems dogs incur as they age. Ulcerations of the tongue or gums also require medical attention, and even extremely bad breath can be a sign or symptom of a disease process.

As you examine your dog's mouth, take notes so that you will more readily remember the things that you need to discuss with your vet or health care professional. The best defense against mouth problems is prevention: Frequent gentle brushing using special toothpaste developed for dogs and a child's soft toothbrush can make all the difference. Regular veterinary dental care is also highly recommended.

Examining the Skin

What better time to examine your dog's skin than during grooming? You can readily become aware of otherwise unnoticed skin conditions by paying close attention to small areas that have lost their fur. Sometimes referred to as "hot spots," these can be a sign of allergies to things that cause skin irritation. For example, some dogs quickly develop allergies to flea bites, which often result in bare spots because the dog constantly chews and scratches at the itchy area for relief.

An excessive amount of dandruff in the coat might indicate

Ear infections are common in dogs with long floppy ears, so examine them often.

Cheyletiella (walking dandruff), which was discussed earlier. This type of dandruff is most visible on the rear of the dog or near the ears.

If you notice tiny black dots in the fur next to the skin, your dog probably has fleas. A number of reliable, safe flea treatments are available through your vet, pet catalogues, or online. Treatment is discussed later in the chapter.

During your all-over check, run your hands

Unusual changes in your dog' behavior or appearance could signal that he is ill.

over your dog's body to see if you can feel lumps or crusty areas under the fur. Most of the time these small lumps are benign, but they do need to be brought to the attention of your vet.

Examining the Feet

Check the feet for wounds, abrasions, or imbedded objects such as thorns. Look between the toes and examine the pads. Whenever your dog is active and moving about, watch for signs of limping, lameness, or incoordination. If he appears to favor one foot over the other, this is an obvious indication of a problem.

General Tips

Always observe your dog for behavioral changes. Has his level of activity changed? Is he lethargic? Has he lost interest in his chewies and toys? A loss of appetite that lasts more than a day is often a sign of an illness. If you suspect that your dog isn't well, check his heart rate and temperature so that you have this information at hand to report to your vet.

Checking Temperature and Heart Rate

Normal temperature for a Cavalier is between 100°F (37.7°C) and 102.5°F (39.2°C). A temperature higher than 104°F is considered an emergency and will require an immediate call to your vet.

To check your dog's temperature, use a digital thermometer, one designed for rectal use. Never use a glass thermometer, and do not place the thermometer in the dog's mouth. Lubricate the thermometer with a small amount of petroleum jelly and gently insert it into the rectum to a depth of approximately 2 inches (5 cm). If possible, place it off to the side of the interior of the rectum to make sure you haven't placed it in stool.

The best place to check your dog's heart rate, or pulse, is on the femoral artery. That artery can easily be palpated inside the rear leg where the leg meets the abdominal area. Count the beats for 15 seconds and then multiply that number by 4 to get the full-minute heart rate. The normal heart rate for an adult Cavalier ranges between 80 and 140 beats per minute (when he is not sleeping).

THE VETERINARIAN

Sometimes you will have already developed a satisfactory relationship with a veterinarian through your ownership of other pets. If this is the case, simply ask your vet if she is comfortable treating Cavaliers. If your vet is familiar with them, there is no reason to change vets simply because you may have changed the breed of dog that you own.

If you do not have a vet, the breeder from whom you purchased your puppy or adult dog may well have recommendations. Other Cavalier owners that you know may recommend their vets, and if the location of their office is suitable, you can certainly consider interviewing them.

Choosing the Right Vet

Many factors must be taken into account to find a vet with whom you can work closely for the good health of your dog. Some of your first concerns should be the proximity of the vet's office; the facilities, services, and emergency arrangements offered; and how well you are able to communicate with the vet and her staff. If you do not feel comfortable in your first meeting with a vet, by all means find another one. The relationship that you form with your dog's health care professional will be long-term, and it is important that you can discuss problems that arise with some degree of comfort. You should be left with the impression that the two of you can work together as a team when it comes to the best interests of your Cavalier. Feel free to discuss costs at the first meeting, and be sure that you have reached a clear understanding of all fees. Make sure that you are clear what the procedure will be should you need the vet after regular office hours or on weekends.

What to Look For

During your first appointment to see a vet, be observant of all aspects of both the facility and its management. If you arrive on time for your appointment, the expectation is that you will not have to wait an inappropriately long time; this, of course, will be determined by you and based on your own personal schedule. The staff should be friendly and patient with you. This is important because you will be seeing these same people each time you visit the vet's office.

Along with a courteous, responsible staff, the clinic should be clean and well maintained. There shouldn't be any animal odors present. Ideally, there should be an entrance into the clinic exclusively set aside for animals who may be suffering from a contagious disease. Your dog should not be forced to come into contact with these animals. Ask questions about the possibility of a necessary overnight stay in the facility in the event that observation, special care, or surgery is required. Find out if attendants will be present overnight. There really is no point in keeping your pet in the facility overnight if he is left alone unmonitored by professionals. He is better off at home, where you are present and can watch him carefully.

Waiting Room Precautions

Anytime you take your dog to the vet clinic, be sure to keep him close to you—either on your lap or in a crate. Cavaliers always feel it is a necessity to meet and mingle, but the vets' office is probably not the best place for that. Interacting freely with the other animals in the waiting room could expose him to other illnesses and to unsettling behavior. Although all the dogs there may usually have lovely temperaments, an animal who is not well may be unhappy enough to snap at the offer of a friendly lick or two from a stranger.

Also consider precautionary measures outside the clinic. If you have driven some distance and feel it necessary to walk your dog for a brief potty break, carry him some distance away from the most obvious pottying locations before you put him down to

Finding a Veterinarian

If you've never owned a dog before, don't worry—finding a vet is easier than you think. Ask everyone you know who has a dog which vet they use and how they like the service. After you've gotten several recommendations, call each practice and explain that you're looking for a vet for your Cavalier. Ask the following questions:

- Does the vet own dogs?
- What are the clinic's regular hours? Does it offer night and weekend appointments?
- Are there boarding and emergency services on-site?
- Is there a vet on-call in case of an after-hours emergency? (If not, what does the clinic recommend that you do with your pet?)
- What are the fees for office visits and vaccinations?
- What are the payment options?

Based on the answers you receive, you can either schedule an appointment with the vet or keep searching.

After your dog's first visit with the vet, ask yourself the following questions:

- Is she compassionate and dedicated to her field of practice?
- Is your dog comfortable with her?
- Are you comfortable with the way she handles your dog?
- Is she experienced with Cavaliers, or at least familiar with Cavalier-specific illnesses?
- Is she open to answering all your questions?
- Is she current on the latest veterinary developments?

Remember that the professional whom you choose will be vital in maintaining the health of your dog. Take your time and find the *right* vet, not just *any* vet.

potty. Remember that a dog with parvo is just as likely to have been walked on the immediate clinic grounds as a healthy dog. After your dog has done his business, pick him up and carry him back to the clinic.

Your Cavalier's First Checkup

At the first visit to your newly chosen vet, expect to fill out some forms about your dog's health history and your billing information. Your vet will need to know the immunization status of your new puppy or adult dog. If at all possible, supply her with the names of the vaccines he's been given, the brand name of the vaccines used, and the exact dates of each vaccination. She will also need to know if your dog has been dewormed and the product used, along with corresponding dates. If a lengthy period of time has elapsed since the dog was last dewormed, your vet may request a stool sample so that she can check for internal parasites. For this reason, it is a good idea to collect a small stool sample in a plastic bag or jar and bring it with you the day of the first visit to the vet.

At the initial exam, your vet will perform a complete physical. She will begin by weighing your dog and checking his vital signs. (If your dog is overweight or underweight, this is a good time to seek her advice regarding weight control.) She will then examine his teeth, ears, and eyes to determine if they appear to be normal and in good condition. She will run her hands through the coat to feel for any lumps, rashes, or open sores on the skin, and check the feet for problems on the pads, toes, or nails. Next she will listen to the heart and lungs and palpate the abdomen. If your dog is an intact male, she will examine the testicles. Often, blood tests are ordered; the results will give your vet a great deal of information about the general overall health of your Cavalier. Although these tests may seem like an unnecessary expense, they are actually a bargain when you consider the great amount of information that is gained from them.

The first visit is also a good time to discuss the use of specific grooming and health care products, such as flea prevention medication. Your vet will have heard of bad reactions to different products and can direct you away from those that may be harmful to your pet. You may also request that your dog's anal glands be checked to make sure that they do not become problematic; anal glands can become infected and burst.

Be sure to give your dog a small treat at the end of the exam so that he will learn to associate visits to the vet with something pleasant. At this time, you can request that the office staff send you a postcard yearly to remind you that it is time for your Cavalier's annual checkup.

Annual Checkups

The initial checkup is just the beginning of the routine health care you will need to provide for your Cavalier. Just because a dog is healthy doesn't mean that you should skip well-dog veterinary visits. It is usually at these annual exams that a vet detects early warning signs of any potentially serious health issue that can affect your Cavalier. Early detection is the best chance for correcting an acute problem or at least slowing its progression. At each annual visit, the vet will also discuss with you any vaccinations that your dog needs.

VACCINATIONS

Vaccinations protect your Cavalier against some of the most deadly diseases that can plague a dog. When a vaccine is administered, it triggers the immune system to develop antibodies that are specific to that disease.

Like people, dogs are most vulnerable to infectious diseases during the first months of life. Newborn puppies receive some immunity from colostrum, an antibody-rich substance produced by the dam's breasts during the first few days after birth. However, this protection is temporary, and sometime between the fifth and tenth weeks, the puppies again become vulnerable to disease. That's why puppies need to be vaccinated.

The traditional approach to puppy vaccination involves giving a series of inoculations beginning at 5 to 8 weeks of age and ending at about 16 weeks, followed by annual boosters. Some vets believe initial vaccines are effective for the life of the dog, while others recommend boosters one year after the puppy series and every three years from then on (except for rabies vaccinations, which must be given according to state laws). Other vets prefer to stagger the booster shots so that they are given about every three years, but only one or two are given per year. Some vets recommend annually checking immunity levels with antibody titers (blood tests to check for immunity levels). Others don't believe that titers are reliable. The best course of action is to educate yourself and discuss with your vet what vaccines your dog needs and when. If you're really uncomfortable with one vet's approach, find another vet.

Most vaccines are injected subcutaneously (under the skin) or intramuscularly (into the muscle), but a few are given in nasal sprays.

Ongoing Controversy

There has been ongoing controversy about the use of vaccines in

Vaccinations help protect a dog against disease.

dogs. In the past, dogs were annually vaccinated against the most common diseases that beset them. For example, rabies vaccines are mandated yearly by individual state laws.

However, there is an ever-increasing sense that vaccines are not always benign and safe. Pet owners and breeders have begun to question why their dogs need to be vaccinated yearly while human children do not, and many vets have noted that they are seeing growing numbers of cases of canine autoimmune disorders. Some suggest that these disorders may be related to both yearly vaccines, as well as to the amount of vaccines and/or treatments given in a single day. Doctor Jean Dodds, whose veterinary practice is in the United States, has researched this issue and now lobbies widely for dog owners to cut down the number of vaccines given to their pets. A simple online search of her name will bring up a lot of information about this controversy.

At the same time, many vets are still firmly in favor of yearly vaccinations. Discuss this issue with your vet, read what Doctor Dodds has to say about it, and then make a decision for your dog that makes the most sense to you personally, based on his health history, your geographic location, and the lifestyle he lives.

Diseases Commonly Vaccinated Against

Veterinary associations have drawn up a list of the diseases that they most often see in their practice and have coordinated the administration of necessary vaccines according to a dog's age, health, and personal activities. The following are the diseases for which dogs are most commonly vaccinated

Bordetellosis (Kennel Cough)

Canine bordetellosis is a bacterial disease of the respiratory tract. Symptoms can include a dry, hacking cough, sneezing and snorting, as well as gagging in response to the cough. You may notice an increase of these symptoms if your dog is wearing a leash because it puts pressure against the airway when the dog is exercising or gets agitated. In some cases, there may be an accompanying fever. The disease lasts 10 to 20 days. Treatment with antibiotics is determined by your vet, but the best treatment is prevention through vaccination.

Because the disease is spread through the air by sneezing or coughing, vaccination is sometimes advised for any dog who will be regularly exposed to other canines at doggy day care, dog parks, or during shows and other events. The vaccine is also often required by dog groomers and is almost always required by professionally run kennels. This is done both to protect your dog and to protect other animals in the kennel.

Bordetellosis is highly contagious, and because of the increased incidence of canine flu, many vets are now recommending that dogs be vaccinated twice yearly.

Coronavirus

Coronavirus causes "enteric" symptoms, meaning symptoms that arise from the gastrointestinal (GI) tract. Specifically, it attacks the lining of the small intestine and causes diarrhea and vomiting. When afflicted by coronavirus, the dog often loses his appetite and fails to eat and drink water, quickly becoming dehydrated. Puppies are at greatest risk of death because of their limited body reserves. Adults have stronger immune systems and will often not have as strong a reaction to the virus.

The most beneficial treatment is the administration of intravenous (IV) fluids with electrolytes, which can treat the dehydration that is the most common cause of death in this disease.

Discuss the need (and frequency) for vaccination with your vet before making a decision about inoculating your dog.

Distemper

Canine distemper is a widespread viral disease of dogs. The symptoms are fever, diarrhea, discharge from the nose and eyes, coughing, sneezing, and loss of appetite. In more advanced cases, paralysis and muscle spasms are possible. This disease is often fatal because no antibiotic directly targets the virus. Diseased animals are most often kept alive with IV fluids to counteract the effects of the dehydration. Distemper is easily transmitted and often fatal.

Vaccination for distemper is always recommended under all circumstances. The highest risk for the disease is to puppies who have not yet been vaccinated. Because they do not yet have a completely developed immune system, exposure often results in death.

Hepatitis

Hepatitis affects dogs worldwide. The virus, canine adenovirus type 1, is shed in the urine, feces, and saliva. It can affect a wide variety of organs, including the liver, kidneys, lungs, and spleen. It can also cause the eye to develop an opaque quality referred to as "blue eye." Symptoms can include fever, bleeding of the

Distemper is a primary killer of unvaccinated dogs. Symptoms include lethargy, fever, diarrhea, and lack of appetite.

Because bacterial diseases are often spread through sneezing or coughing, vaccination is sometimes advised for dogs who will be regularly exposed to other canines at doggy day care, dog parks, or during shows and other events.

gums and other soft tissue areas, and decreased white blood cell count. The disease can be fatal, and for those who recover there may be long-term effects such as chronic hepatitis. Recovery is often slow. Treatment often includes antibiotics to prevent further complications, vitamin supplements, and nondairy fluids to soothe an inflamed throat. Discuss appropriate treatment modalities with your vet.

Hepatitis virus often stays alive for months, so it can be easily transmitted among dogs and contracted at locations where they have urinated such as yards, play parks, and along popular dog walking paths.

Leptospirosis

Leptospirosis is a bacterial disease that can infect all warm-blooded animals, including humans. It can result from contact with the urine and other body secretions of affected animals. Aside from direct contact, environmental sources can also expose individuals to the bacteria. For example, water sources such as rivers can become contaminated and infect individuals through open sores or wounds. Common symptoms are fever, severe loss of appetite, depression, and generalized body pain.

Because many different *Leptospira* pathogens can cause leptospirosis, your vet can best advise you as to the necessary vaccination protocols, particularly if your dog lives in an area in which he has access to wild animals. Treatment generally consists of antibiotics to kill the bacteria and adjunct therapies such as IV fluids to counteract the dehydration that can result with anorexia.

Caution is always advised when handling an animal infected with leptospirosis because transmission to humans can result from direct contact with broken skin or mucous membranes. In fact, veterinarians are the largest group of humans to contract the disease.

Lyme Disease

Lyme disease is a bacterial infection spread to dogs and humans through the bite of an infected deer tick. It has been reported throughout the United States. It is often missed as a diagnosis because some animals exhibit no symptoms at all. When symptoms are present they may include fever, loss of appetite, lethargy, vomiting, and joint pain. Long-term infection in dogs can lead to heart disease, kidney damage, or personality/neurological disorders such as aggression, confusion, and even seizures. Discuss treatment with your vet, who will be up-to-date on which antibiotics are working best with the current strain of Lyme disease.

As the incidence of the disease grows, vaccination is being recommended by vets. Both inoculation and the use of regularly

Both inoculation and the use of regularly applied tick preventive medications are useful in protecting your dog against Lyme disease.

applied tick preventative medications are useful in protecting your pet.

Parainfluenza

Parainfluenza is a viral infection of the upper respiratory tract. In some cases, it may progress to pneumonia, which can be life-threatening. Symptoms include a hacking cough, fever, loss of appetite, and lethargy. Highly contagious, the disease is most common among dogs who are often around other dogs because it is airborne and spreads easily through coughing or sneezing.

Because parainfluenza is caused by several viruses, no specific antibiotic is given for treatment. As with other viral diseases that debilitate the dog to the point where he no longer can eat or drink, IV fluids are often ordered. The goal is to support the dog's body while his immune system fights the virus. Discuss vaccination with your vet.

Parvovirus

Canine parvovirus (CPV), commonly called "parvo," is a widely spread, deadly disease universally feared by owners, particularly those of puppies. While adult dogs can contract parvo, it is more frequently found in the puppy population. Often the onset of the disease is rapid. The first symptom noticed is bloody diarrhea; this initial episode of diarrhea is alarming as it consists primarily of blood rather than feces. The dog will also be lethargic, visibly ill, and eventually anorexic due to continual diarrhea, vomiting, and fever.

Parvo is often fatal but death is usually due to dehydration, which damages the kidneys and can cause the heart to develop dangerous arrhythmias. Because it is viral, no antibiotics can be relied upon to cure the disease. IV therapy is of utmost importance to prevent dehydration. In some cases, vets have also successfully treated parvo with the blood of dogs who have survived the disease. The blood is drawn, spun down into a clear serum, and administered through an IV. If your puppy is infected, discuss this option with your vet who may have a record of dogs he has treated with the disease.

Immunization is vitally important to prevent outbreaks of parvo. Check with your breeder to make sure that your puppy was immunized prior to taking him home.

Rabies

Rabies is a highly contagious, virus-borne disease that can affect warm-blooded animals, including humans. The wildlife population represents the largest source of the infection, which is transmitted through saliva and bites. The virus affects the nervous system and causes symptoms that are usually behavioral, such as aggression or withdrawal. Depending on the type of rabies, advanced symptoms can include light sensitivity, facial tics, stomach upset, and loss of muscle coordination. Once the symptoms of the disease appear, the disease is always fatal. There is no treatment for canine rabies.

The best way to prevent rabies is through vaccination. Each state in the United States has its own vaccination protocols, ranging from inoculation once a year to once every three years. Some foreign countries do not have a history of rabies, which is why they will not allow importation of dogs from the United States.

Puppies are not generally vaccinated until they are 4 to 6 months old, so owners should expect to be responsible for the first vaccination. Your vet will be familiar with the protocol for your state. You must provide proof of vaccinations for licensing your dog and also before flying on any airline with your dog.

SHOULD YOU BREED YOUR CAVALIER?

Dogs should never be bred for casual reasons. The financial incentive to sell puppies is a poor and selfish excuse for breeding, and dogs should never be bred to teach children responsibility or to give them an at-home experience of the "joy of birth." Breeding is a serious undertaking that requires extensive expertise, time, and money.

Breeders choose to breed their dogs for valid and worthwhile reasons. Many do so to focus their breeding programs on improving the look and structure of their breed in order to bring it closer to the breed standard. Others may choose to concentrate on improving the health of the breed through careful selection and vigilance in testing for diseases and genetic problems. Both of these goals are long-term and take many years to accomplish. Producing more dogs in a society that is already overburdened with unwanted or abandoned animals who are euthanized each year is not an endeavor to be taken lightly.

The decision to breed your Cavalier should not be taken lightly. Breeding is a serious undertaking that requires extensive expertise, time, and money.

Spaying and Neutering

Spaying and neutering are both relatively simple surgeries that will prevent your Cavalier from being used for breeding. The correct term for the procedure is "spay" for females and "neuter" for males.

Spaying

A female not intended for showing or breeding should be spayed at approximately 6 months of age. Your goal should be to have her spayed before her first "heat" or "season," which is prior to the time she develops breast tissue. This is because the development of breast tissue will leave her at risk for breast cancer for the remainder of her life.

Spaying is a relatively simple procedure. Reproductive organs are removed through a small incision made on the abdomen. This leaves only a very small scar that is almost invisible after healing is completed. Your dog may be uncomfortable the day of the surgery, and possibly the day after, but the pain is minimal. The wound closure that your vet chooses may be a dissolving suture or surgical glue, but you may be required to return to the vet for a postsurgical exam and removal depending on the suture type. Do not postpone the removal of the sutures because infection at the site can occur as a result of the delay.

Neutering

Males who are not intended to be used for breeding should be "neutered" prior to reaching 6 months of age. Neutering a male will often prevent him from developing the bad habit of "marking" his territory: lifting his leg and releasing small drops of urine. This behavioral trait is associated with male hormones. If a dog is neutered prior to reaching puberty, many of the unwanted behaviors associated with the triggering of these hormones will not occur.

For male dogs, the neutering procedure consists of removing the testicles. Because removal of the testicles, or "castration," is viewed by humans as an issue fraught with emotional and societal implications, many dog owners are very resistant to the concept of neutering their dogs. Yet, for some reason these very dog owners do not appear to have the same emotional reaction to spaying females. However, dogs do not have the same thought processes that humans do, and neutering a male will make him a better companion and house pet.

The surgical site may be somewhat painful the day of the surgery and perhaps the day after, but it heals quickly. Once healed, dogs do not appear to know the difference. Neutering will decrease marking, aggressive behaviors, and sexual activities with other animals and toys.

Discuss the recommended age for spaying and neutering your pet with your vet. If possible, schedule the procedure on a Friday so that you can be home for the first couple of days of your dog's recovery.

PARASITES

Parasites fall into two groups: internal parasites, which live inside the body, and external parasites, which live outside the body. Both can cause your dog discomfort, and some can be dangerous if left untreated. Your vet can tell you which ones to be most concerned about and what treatments are recommended.

Internal Parasites

Worms are the most common internal parasites of dogs, with roundworms (ascarids) being the type from which dogs suffer most frequently. Other types of the same variety (nematodes) are hookworms and whipworms.

Even puppies from the cleanest kennels can have worms. Prevention is difficult; in their larval stage, worms cannot be eradicated because they are not susceptible to the various forms of deworming medications. Some worms become encysted within the dam's body in a larval state years before she was bred; they could have become well entrenched in her body tissue even when she herself was a puppy. Larvae are only activated by the hormonal changes that occur during gestation. Once activated, it is thought that the larvae pass from the mother to her puppies in her milk. Usually, breeders will routinely worm puppies and mothers at the same time. Your breeder should provide you with such information at the time of the purchase.

If your vet discovers that your puppy or adult dog has worms, she will prescribe an effective, safe medication and provide you with clear instructions regarding its use. Avoid the kinds of deworming medications you can buy at supermarket and pet stores. When it comes to internal parasites, follow your vet's advice.

Heartworms

Heartworms are deadly parasites transmitted from dog to dog through mosquito bites. They are the most deadly of all internal parasites.

At your first visit with the vet, discuss the incidence of heartworm infestation in your area. Carefully follow her prevention protocol and the medication regime she prescribes to the letter to prevent future problems. The best precaution to take in the case of heartworm infestation is prevention because treatment of an already infected dog is expensive and risky. If you have problems administering the pills that are prescribed, try placing them inside

Deworming Caution

Do not routinely deworm a dog simply as a preventive measure. The best course of action to take regarding deworming is to provide the vet with a stool sample and then follow the exact instructions that she gives you. Medications other than those prescribed should not be used, and those approved by your vet should only be administered as directed. Deworming medications are, after all, poisons and need to be regarded as such.

of a small ball of sausage. It is a rare dog who will refuse a yummy treat, even if it contains a pill.

Hookworms

Hookworms are very small, thin worms that attach themselves to the wall of the dog's intestine in order to feed on his blood. In doing so, they can cause anemia, with its accompanying weakness and decreased stamina. Other symptoms include bloody diarrhea, dark stools, pale skin coloration, and skin that is red and swollen, usually at the feet where the larvae have penetrated. Dogs infested with hookworms do not thrive, no matter how much they eat. As a result, they may exhibit weight loss and suffer eventual malnutrition.

Hookworms are transmitted through infected feces, although they cannot be seen in stool. The vet will have to examine a stool sample under a microscope to identify the eggs. A number of medications are available for treatment and to prevent reinfestation.

Roundworms

Roundworms are the most common type of canine worm. They are sometimes visible in stool, and at a glance they resemble cooked spaghetti. If the mother ever had roundworms, puppies can become infested in utero because the larvae can migrate to their lungs during gestation. It could also be encysted in her body and passed on through her milk when the puppies nurse.

Once in the body, the larvae find their way to the intestines and can grow up to five inches (13 cm) in length. They can cause a pot-bellied appearance and will often slow the rate of growth. Adult dogs who are infested may lose their appetites and vomit following meals. Treatment is easy to administer and rarely causes negative side effects.

Whipworms

Whipworms, also common to dogs, are rarely visible to the naked eye. They look a little bit like a piece of thread with an enlarged end. These parasites attach themselves to the lower part of the small intestine to feed and can live there for months or years. Symptoms are not as apparent as with other types of worms, which makes them hard to detect, but whipworms are often diagnosed in dogs who have chronic weight loss and failure to thrive,

coupled with stools that appear to be covered in mucous. Repeat deworming may be necessary to treat this infestation, so be vigilant about follow-ups with your vet.

Tapeworms

Also quite common, tapeworms (cestodes) are a different variety of internal parasite because they require two different hosts during their life cycle. Tapeworm larvae are transmitted to affected dogs by intermediate hosts such as fleas. Dogs become infected when they ingest the infected host containing flea larvae. Once ingested or transmitted, the larvae grow into adult tapeworms inside the body and can grow several feet (meters) long. Sometimes fatal, tapeworms feed on digested food, robbing your dog of nutrition.

Tapeworms can be hard to detect because dogs usually don't show symptoms. They are diagnosed when they are seen on fresh stool as flat, white worm segments, or more frequently visualized like grains of rice near the rectal area. Your vet will diagnose and recommend treatment for this type of worm. The best precaution is to prevent tapeworm infestation by keeping your dog flea-free.

External Parasites

External parasites such as fleas, mites, fungi (like ringworm),

External parasites such as fleas, mites, and fungi can make your Cavalier uncomfortable and potentially sick. Check your dog for fleas and ticks after he's been playing outdoors.

and ticks can make your Cavalier uncomfortable and potentially sick. They can be found anywhere on the body.

Parasite prevention often means introducing insecticides into your Cavalier's system, the long-term effects of which concern many dog owners. No documentation suggests that long-term pesticide use poses health risks, but there is plenty of information on the dangers of parasite-borne diseases. Talk to your vet about the safest and best course of parasite prevention for your dog.

Fleas

Fleas are by far the most difficult external parasite to eliminate. Not only do they reproduce incredibly fast, but they actually can become resistant to insecticides. To check your Cavalier for fleas, separate a patch of his fur to examine the skin. If you notice tiny black flecks that resemble ground pepper, that's flea "dirt," or excrement. If your dog scratches excessively, it could also be a symptom of a flea infestation. Some dogs have allergic reactions to flea bites that make them utterly miserable. Seek prompt veterinary attention to treat the skin irritation, and get instructions on how to rid your home of these pests.

Mites

Two types of body mites—sarcoptic and demodex—can affect your dog, and a vet's examination will determine what kind is present and the best treatment. In general, she will prescribe medicine to kill the mites and their eggs and to heal the dermatological damage they caused.

- Sarcoptic mites can cause big skin problems for your dog by causing sarcoptic mange, making his skin itchy and crusty and raising little bumps.
- Demodex mites, which infest the hair follicles, cause follicular or demodectic mange, which may or may not cause itching. It will cause bare patches in your dog's fur and give him a moth-eaten appearance.

Ringworm

Ringworm is not really a worm but a highly contagious fungus that spreads easily among animals and humans through contact with infected skin, hair, or soil. Infective spores are constantly dropped off the hair and skin of infected dogs or people, and

contact with even one spore is all it takes to catch it. Ringworm fungi feed on dead surface skin and hair cells, causing an irritating itch that develops into a scaly or raw-looking bald patch.

Ringworm is difficult to eliminate as the fungi can be very tenacious. It can live for years in the environment and resist treatment, which usually involves a combination of topical and systemic medication. Impeccable hygiene and decontamination of the dog's environment must be practiced until the vet declares the dog ringworm-free.

Adult humans with compromised immune systems and children are most susceptible; if your Cavalier is diagnosed with ringworm, and you don't have it at that time, chances are you won't catch it.

Ticks

Ticks are arachnids who feed off their host's blood by burrowing their mouths into the skin. More than merely a nuisance, ticks can carry disease. As discussed earlier, the tiny deer tick is especially known to carry Lyme disease, a flu-like illness that causes fatigue, fever, loss of appetite, and swollen neck glands. Humans and dogs are susceptible to this debilitating disease. Ticks also carry Rocky Mountain spotted fever, which can cause paralysis in dogs.

Ticks come in many sizes and colors, from brown to almost blue, and are pretty easy to see on a Cavalier's short coat. When

Safe Tick Removal

When it comes to removing ticks, you get all sorts of advice—some of it is not good advice. Never do the following:

- Do not use a sharp implement.
- Do not crush, puncture, or squeeze the tick's body.
- Do not apply substances to the tick like petroleum jelly, gasoline, or lidocaine. These "folk" remedies are supposed to make the tick pull out of the host, but studies show them to be ineffective.
- Do not apply a hot match or heated nail to the tick. The theory is that the tick will be burned and pull out of the host. Even if this method works, the risk of burning your dog is too great.
- Do not pull the tick out with a twisting or jerking action.
- Do not handle the tick with your bare hands.

removing a tick, don't do anything that may rupture or squeeze the tick's body (such as using a hot matchstick or a needle to puncture the tick) and exude any potentially infectious fluids. The simplest, safest way to remove a tick is to pull it out with a pair of blunt tweezers dedicated to the task. Grasp the tick as close to its head as possible, pull it out with a steady movement, and flush it down the toilet. If part of the tick's head remains attached to the dog's body, apply an antiseptic to the site. The head will eventually fall off.

COMMON HEALTH ISSUES

Thanks to advances in veterinary medicine and conscientious health care on the part of owners, dogs are now living longer, healthier lives. However, during the course of their lifetime, common health issues may arise. Knowing how to recognize potential problems and how to handle them is important to your dog' overall well-being.

Allergies

Allergies have reached epidemic proportions, in both animals and humans, and they can make us feel very uncomfortable. Although they cannot be cured, they can be managed with patience and determination. Medical treatments include antihistamines and steroids, which are effective for occasional flare-ups. For ongoing allergy problems, though, Cavalier owners should investigate other means of treatment, such as immunotherapy. Immunotherapy is designed to desensitize the dog to the allergen by building up immunity to it through injections containing small amounts of the allergen itself or extracts from it. Many dogs respond quite well to this treatment.

Allergies can be grouped into four categories: contact, flea, food, and inhalant (atopic).

Contact Allergy

Contact allergies cause reactions when the dog physically touches a substance containing the allergen. Some of the more common contact allergens are plastic, grass, and wool. Sometimes allergy shots can combat the uncomfortable symptoms, but lifestyle changes are often necessary. These kinds of changes can be as simple as substituting a stainless steel food bowl for a plastic one or as creative as making an alternative outdoor surface for rest and

Like humans, dogs can be allergic to many things, such as certain ingredients in food.

relaxation (other than grass).

Flea Allergy

The most common type of dog allergy, flea allergy isn't an allergy to the flea itself but to a protein in its saliva, which remains in the skin after a bite. Severe reactions can cause irritations that make the dog feel miserable and bald patches that make him look just as bad. Your vet will recommend the best way to rid your home and dog of the fleas and eggs, as well as prescribe a medication to heal the skin irritations and prevent infection.

Food Allergy

Food allergies in dogs are often caused by the same foods that cause them in humans: soy, milk products, eggs, wheat, corn, and chicken. The most likely reaction is itchy, irritated skin, although vomiting and diarrhea also can occur. Food allergies are identified only by trial and error, which can take some time. Once the offending allergen is isolated, it's not difficult to customize your Cavalier's diet.

Inhalant (Atopic) Allergy

Another common type of allergy, inhalant or atopic allergies result when an allergic dog breathes in an offending allergen, such as tobacco smoke, pollen, or mold spores. Even if an allergic dog stays indoors all the time, outside allergens can find their way into the house and your dog's nose. Treatment varies, depending on allergic manifestation, but elimination of the allergen is the first step. Your vet will then discuss with you whether allergy shots, antihistamines, or topical skin treatment is in order.

Diarrhea

Diarrhea can result from just about anything. Some of the causes are very benign while others are serious and life-threatening. Although Cavaliers are very easily enticed to eat just about anything, they seem to require a bit more time to adjust to new foods. Even a water change can cause diarrhea—a single potato chip can cause a Cavalier to have diarrhea! Nervousness, stress, overeating, internal parasites, and any number of viral or bacterial organisms are all possible causes.

If you feel that your dog's diarrhea is caused by overeating, or having new food or water, treat the condition at home by restricting food intake and cutting down access to water for 24 hours. To prevent dehydration, provide ice cubes or large ice chips; Cavaliers often enjoy them more than water anyway. Because diarrhea is actually a result of an inflamed bowel, you should keep your dog on a bland diet of rice, cooked macaroni, cottage cheese, or a combination of all of these for a few days to give the inflammation of the bowel wall time to heal.

A dog who has bloody diarrhea or diarrhea accompanied by a fever or vomiting lasting more than a day should be seen by your vet.

Knowing how to recognize potential health problems and how to handle them is important to your dog's overall well-being.

Vomiting

All dogs vomit at one time or another. Dogs who eat grass will often vomit shortly after ingesting it. This shouldn't cause great concern. Puppies and younger dogs will often vomit if they overeat, particularly if they run and rough-house following a big meal. This can usually be prevented by either crating the dog for a while after he's fed or feeding him smaller meals more frequently throughout the day.

If your Cavalier vomits immediately after eating, this could be a symptom of gastrointestinal obstruction. Vomiting that recurs over a period of time could be an indication of a foreign object in the stomach or an actual illness of the stomach. Persistent vomiting of this type requires a trip to the vet. If your dog is vomiting in this manner, withhold food and give only small amounts of water until he can be examined. If the vomit is a foul-smelling substance that resembles feces, this is a life-threatening emergency because it could indicate an intestinal blockage. If the vomit is a substance that looks like coffee grounds, it is almost certainly a sign of a GI bleed of some type. Vomiting red blood is even more of an emergency.

Sometimes vomiting is a simple one-time event that is relatively insignificant. Sometimes it is a symptom of a serious illness that requires professional diagnosis and treatment. If in doubt, call the vets' office and describe exactly what you are seeing and let your vet decide if a visit is necessary.

Butt Scooting

While not particularly charming, "butt scooting" may not necessarily be an indication that your dog has worms but rather a simple form of entertainment—for your benefit not his. One can only assume that because Cavaliers tend to scoot their butts in front of company and are especially active during the dinner hour, our little darlings have determined that this is an activity viewed fondly by one and all. Cavaliers are Olympians when it comes to butt scooting, and there appears to be very little that you can do to discourage it. If the behavior persists, it is more likely to be an indication of inflamed anal glands, so take your dog to the vet and have him check for this condition.

Urinary Tract Diseases

Bladder and kidney infections can exhibit symptoms that are very subtle or very dramatic. If your Cavalier appears to be lethargic, shows a loss of appetite, and has a temperature, he could have a urinary tract infection (UTI). If it appears that he has a difficult time urinating or if he appears to be in pain while urinating, it is almost certain that he has a UTI. Frequent urination or releasing just a few drops is also a possible sign of a UTI.

If you suspect that your Cavalier has a UTI, walk him in an area that will allow you to see his urine after he evacuates his bladder, or collect a small amount of urine in a clear container or on a clean, white cloth. If the urine is cloudy or bloody, an infection of the kidney, urethra, bladder, or prostate gland is a certainty. Your vet will need to examine your dog and collect urine so that she can begin the assessment process to determine how best to cure the infection. If a male has repeated infections of the urinary tract, it may be necessary to neuter him if you have not already done so. You cannot treat a UTI yourself. It will require the skills of your vet.

DISEASES COMMON TO CAVALIERS

Almost all purebred dogs and breed groups are more prone to certain health conditions than others. This is probably due to the fact that one or more dogs used for breeding early on in the breed's history were affected by the disease. In general, the Cavalier is a hearty little dog. However, keep in mind that no breed is disease-free, and any breed can develop any ailment. The following are diseases that may affect your Cavalier.

Mitral Valve Disease

As we discussed in Chapter 1, Cavaliers are something of an engineered, or reconstructed, breed. It is thought that all Cavaliers can trace their roots back to at least one or two of six dogs. Sadly for the breed, at least one of these six dogs had the genetics for mitral valve disease (MVD). When those six dogs were interbred, the genetic load for MVD became very strong, and by the early 1980s it was discovered that 50 percent of all Cavaliers who had reached the age of 5 had MVD as evidenced by mitral regurgitation. In the early 1990s, researchers studied the disease in Cavaliers in the United States and found that 50 percent of

all 4 year old Cavaliers had mitral regurgitation. As might be expected, in both studies, it was found that the older the Cavalier got, the more severe the disease became.

MVD is clearly genetic in nature. However, it is not inherited in a simple dominant/recessive gene mode. Studies have shown that MVD requires the interaction of several different gene pairs. This mode of genetic transmission is called polygenetic; when a certain number of the devastating gene pairs are present, a dog will eventually develop the disease. Because of the polygenetic nature of MVD, its occurrence is more difficult to predict and much more difficult to "breed out" than diseases that are genetically based on a simple dominant/recessive pattern.

What Is MVD?

The canine heart has four chambers and four one-way valves. The upper chambers are the left and right atriums. The atriums are the collection vessels for blood that is returning from its journey through the body back to the heart. The lower chambers are the left and right ventricles. The ventricles receive the blood and pump it back out of the heart and through the body. The mitral valve is the valve between the left atrium and the left ventricle. When the heart is functioning as it should, this valve shuts as the left ventricle contracts and then blood is projected through the aorta into the circulatory system.

When a dog has MVD, the tissue that makes up the mitral valve begins to shrink and curl, losing its elasticity and hence its ability to close tightly. Because the valve no longer closes tightly, and a gap is left between the left atrium and the left ventricle, blood is able to flow backward into the left atrium when the left ventricle contracts. This backflow of blood from the ventricle is called mitral regurgitation. While blood is flowing backward into the atrium, there is less blood volume to be pumped out into the body. The left atrium enlarges to accommodate the increased blood volume being forced back into it on each beat of the heart, and the left ventricle expands to meet the demands placed upon it by the faulty mitral valve. This taxes both chambers of the heart. As the disease worsens, the entire left side of the heart enlarges, and the dog may exhibit signs and symptoms of congestive heart failure. Fluid may begin to accumulate in the lungs. This accumulation of fluid in the lungs together with the pressure from the enlarged heart on the

bronchial tubes leads to coughing.

In most dogs, the very first symptom of MVD is exercise intolerance. However, when your dog is basically your little couch companion, you may not notice a loss of tolerance for energetic running and playing. You will, however, notice coughing. Your Cavalier's respiration rate may increase and his breathing may appear to be labored. He may have to work much harder to get air into his lungs. Some dogs may even faint because of the inability of the weakened heart to pump enough blood into the brain. No one can predict the pattern that MVD will follow. Sometimes the symptoms will progress very slowly over several years, and at other times the symptoms may progress very rapidly and a dog will die shortly after diagnosis.

Diagnosis of MVD

The first diagnosis of MVD can be made by listening to the heart with a stethoscope. Mitral regurgitation is heard as a heart murmur. Once a murmur is detected, other tests are ordered such as X-rays or echocardiograms. These more advanced tests are best performed by a canine cardiologist, which often means traveling to a veterinary teaching hospital.

Unfortunately for those of us who own and love Cavaliers, there is currently no cure for MVD and no way to prevent it. The disease continues to worsen, although the rate of deterioration varies from dog to dog. Some affected dogs continue to live long lives, while others die early. Overweight dogs may certainly benefit from a weight-loss program. Drugs can help to alleviate some of MVD's symptoms, particularly diuretics, which assist in the removal of fluid from the lungs, and vasodilators, which expand the blood vessels for better circulation.

What Does the Future Hold for MVD?

There is never enough funding for canine disease research. However, several organizations are working toward curing canine diseases, two of which are the American Kennel Club's (AKC) Canine Health Project and the Morris Animal Foundation. We can each do our part by contributing to these organizations in the hope that one day the genes responsible for causing MVD will be identified. Once identified, dogs who are carriers of this devastating disease can be removed from breeding programs so

that this debilitating disease can be but an unpleasant memory. This is the hope of every Cavalier fancier in the world.

Hip Dysplasia

Canine hip dysplasia (CHD), or the malformation of the hip joint, occurs in approximately 10 to 12 percent of all Cavaliers; although it is generally associated with larger breeds, toy breeds are affected by it as well.

If CHD is detected while a dog is still young, it is thought to be genetic in nature, but it can also occur as a natural result of the aging process in older dogs. If a Cavalier 1 year of age is diagnosed with CHD, genetics is probably the cause. If a Cavalier doesn't show signs of CHD until 7 years of age, aging is probably the cause. Generally speaking, if hip dysplasia is diagnosed at a young age, the symptoms will be more severe; if it doesn't appear until the dog is older, the symptoms will be milder in nature.

CHD occurs when the femur, the leg bone of the thigh, doesn't fit snugly into the socket of the pelvis. Common symptoms are a general inability to tolerate exercise, stiffness, and limping. The affected dog may have difficulty rising from a position on the floor, he may display a reluctance to climb stairs, and his gait may be abnormal. Over time, CHD will cause arthritic changes in the joint.

Hip dysplasia can make moving around painful for a Cavalier.

Treatment can range from increasing exercise to the use of anti-inflammatory medications. If the dog is severely affected, surgery may be needed. Discuss the various options with your vet when the condition is first diagnosed.

Patellar Luxation

Cavaliers also carry the genes for patellar luxation, which is the displacement of the kneecap or patella. Patellar luxation can also occur as a result of injury or accident. If the knee cap "pops" or slips out of the correct position, the dog will be unable to straighten out his leg. He will hold his leg up, usually for a brief period of time, although sometimes for extended periods. When a dog with patellar luxation is examined while in a standing position, the affected leg may be bowed inward or outward. Very mild cases do not require anything but vigilance, a watchful eye, and more frequent vet examinations to track the progress of the disease. More severe cases will require surgery. Discuss these options with your vet when the problem is first diagnosed.

EMERGENCY CARE

It can never be overstated that being prepared for an emergency can save your Cavalier's life in certain situations. So, before you bring home your puppy or adult Cavalier, begin gathering the materials and products that you will need for a good quality medical kit. Begin by obtaining a safe container for your emergency canine medical supplies. A small fishing tackle box works nicely. These are usually inexpensive and have several small compartments that offer good visibility for the contents within. They also close securely and can often be locked, a necessary feature if you have small children. If you do lock your emergency kit, keep it in the same place at all times and tape or hang the key high up on a wall or inside the door of the storage location.

Canine Emergency Medical Kit

Here are some of the items that you will need to keep in an emergency medical kit for your dog. The list may change from time to time if your dog develops a specific health issue, but these products represent a reasonably well-equipped kit. Apart from the supplies needed, write the phone numbers of your vet's office, an emergency veterinary clinic, and the Animal Poison Control Center

Every responsible pet owner should arm herself with emergency first-aid information that could save a pet in need of immediate medical attention.

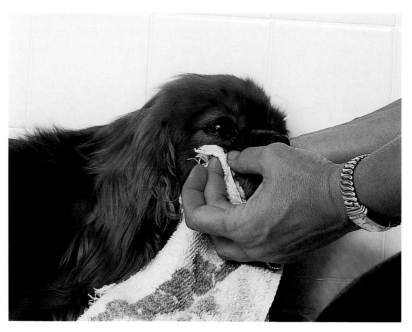

in your area on the box lid in indelible marker pen, and keep an instruction sheet inside the box that provides guidance for any special needs your dog may have.

You kit should contain:

- antibiotic ointment
- antidiarrhea medication (per vet's recommendation)
- canine first aid book
- eye ointment (per vet's recommendation)
- hydrogen peroxide (never put into the eyes)
- latex gloves
- liquid antibacterial soap
- liquid Betadine
- saline eye wash
- scissors (blunt end)
- self-activating cold compresses or a small ice bag
- self-sticking bandages (such as vet wrap)
- several small washcloths
- small flashlight
- small magnifying glass if needed
- sterile applicators or swabs
- sterile gauze dressings
- stethoscope (inexpensive; optional)

- super glue (only for use in suturing, or gluing together, a cleaned wound in an extreme emergency when you are simply unable to get to a vet or emergency facility right away)
- syringes for the oral administration of medication
- tweezers

After using any of your emergency "tools," wash them well in hot water and a good-quality antibacterial soap and allow them to air dry before replacing them into the emergency medical kit.

Emergency Treatment

You can only take a few steps in the event that you face an emergency situation with your dog, but they are important and life-saving steps. In all cases, call ahead to let the vet know that you are coming in for an emergency and describe what has happened to the office staff. They may divert you to an emergency veterinary clinic specializing in emergencies.

Next, make sure that your dog's airway is clear and protected. Remove his collar and position his head in a way that best enables him to breathe. Apply pressure to any area that is bleeding; plain clean towels placed on a wound often work well for this. Keep your dog warm, if possible.

Talk to your dog in a calm, controlled manner. Cavaliers, in particular, are very intuitive and in tune with your mood. Staying calm will help your dog not to panic, which can be a further inducement to go into shock. If you suspect that bones are broken, move your dog carefully, using either a board of some kind or a blanket sling. Almost everyone has a large bread cutting board, which can be used to move a dog the size of a Cavalier. A hard plastic storage box lid can also be used. Moving an injured dog

Normal Vital Signs

- A dog's normal temperature is 99.5°F to 102.8°F.
- A dog's normal heart rate is 60 to 120 beats per minute.
- A dog normally takes 14 to 22 breaths per minute.

187

carelessly can cause further damage and unnecessary pain. When your dog is ready to be moved, transport him as quickly as possible to the vet's office.

FIRST AID

Every dog owner should have at least a basic knowledge of first aid. Although our vets and the services they provide are a vital and necessary part of the life of our pets, they cannot be with us 24 hours a day. Knowing what to do in an emergency and keeping a well-stocked first-aid kit may end up saving your Cavalier's life one day.

Airway/Breathing Obstruction

If your dog is unable to breathe, this is a life-threatening situation that needs immediate attention. If he is unable to breathe at all, open his mouth and see if an object is blocking his airway; use a flashlight if necessary. Often dogs get a ball or toy caught in their throat that occludes the airway. Death will occur very quickly in this situation, so begin emergency treatment by administering the Heimlich maneuver. Hold your dog up and apply quick upward thrusts under the rib cage. If this does not dislodge the foreign object, use every method available to you to attempt to remove it from his throat. Try holding him upside down and administering a few short "whacks" to the back to see if that will release it. If you can see the object but cannot reach it, you might try holding your dog upside down and actually applying a small amount of pressure to the throat behind the object.

If your dog is breathing but gasping and has his head extended, he is in trouble. He will be very anxious, but this will soon progress to weakness and eventually unconsciousness. Open your dog's mouth and sweep your fingers from side to side as far down as you can reach to remove secretions or possible foreign bodies. Using a washcloth or any other piece of available fabric, try to grasp the tongue and pull it forward. (It will be almost impossible to hold the tongue without using a fabric of some sort to hang on to it.) If the airway is still somewhat open, you can try mouth-to-mouth resuscitation. Seal the dog's mouth with your hands and blow gently into his nose until his chest expands for three seconds and then stop. Keep doing this until the dog breathes on his own. In all these situations, get your dog to the vet as soon as possible.

Poisoning

The three most common poisons that your dog will encounter are rat or mouse poison, snail bait, and automobile antifreeze. Other gardening and cleaning substances may also be dangerous if ingested. Dogs will also eat any human pills that they find.

Whenever you purchase gardening products for your yard, read the labels carefully. Poisonous substances may be placed in neighborhood gardens without your knowledge, and your dog may encounter them while giving his environment the usual sniff test during his daily walk. Make every effort to encourage your dog to stay on the sidewalk during walks, and do not allow him to wander off into unfamiliar yards, which is also a courtesy to your neighbors. Many plants are poisonous to dogs as well, so it just makes good sense to train your dog to stay on the sidewalk for outings.

Antifreeze is highly toxic to dogs, and it must be quite palatable to them because they gravitate toward it if they have the opportunity. It is common for radiators to leak antifreeze onto driveways and parking areas. You can easily recognize it by its clear, chartreuse color. If you suspect your dog has ingested this or any other toxic substance or human medication, take him to the vet

Poisonous substances may be placed in neighborhood gardens without your knowledge, so encourage your dog to stay on the sidewalk during walks and do not allow him to wander off unsupervised.

immediately. Also bring the suspicious substance with you and the container in which it came.

Poisons work very quickly, so it is urgent that you take your dog to the vet for diagnosis and treatment at the first sign of poisoning. If you are unable to get there or to reach the office staff by phone, call the Animal Poison Control Center at (888) 426-4435 for instructions.

In a dire emergency, attempt to induce vomiting by administering a solution of half a cup (120 ml) of water mixed with half a cup (120 ml) of hydrogen peroxide or a cup (240 ml) of water with one full tablespoon (15 ml) of salt mixed in until dissolved. Do not induce vomiting if your dog has eaten:

- acids
- alkalis
- cleaning solvents
- petroleum products
- sharp objects
- tranquilizers

Do not attempt to induce vomiting if your dog is having convulsions, is very lethargic, or is in a coma. If it has been over two hours since he ingested the poisonous substance, it has already passed through the stomach, so induced vomiting is of no use. Activated charcoal is a product that may be helpful at this point because it can absorb a variety of toxic substances. It can easily be kept in your emergency medical kit.

You can try other counteractive measures. If your dog is awake and willing to drink or eat, try diluting the ingested poison by giving him equal amounts of milk and vegetable oil (or egg whites). If your dog has swallowed an acidic product, giving baking soda mixed in water or Milk of Magnesia to neutralize the acid. If he has ingested an alkaline poison, an acid given orally is helpful, although it is extremely hard to make a dog drink lemon juice or vinegar. Be warned also that forcing your dog to take products of that kind can create aspiration pneumonia if he vomits up his stomach contents and some goes into his lungs.

Generally, in all cases of poisoning, it is always best to take your dog to the vet for diagnosis and treatment as soon as possible

Seizure Activity

Many things can cause seizures in dogs, but if you witness a dog

having a seizure you must act immediately and not worry about the cause until much later.

The first thing you must do is get all other dogs away from the area immediately. For some reason, dogs become very aggressive when seeing another dog who is hurt or sick, displaying what appears to be a "kick 'em while they're down" mentality. Even Cavaliers, as good-natured and sweet as they are, will often become somewhat hostile toward another dog who is on the ground.

During a seizure, a dog may be awake or appear to be sleeping. He also may be drooling excessively and will probably be lying on his side exhibiting stiffness and muscle spasms. To both protect him from the effects of his convulsions and to reassure him that he is safe, wrap him in a blanket or large towel. Protect yourself from the dog too. Although he may not intend to, he may bite you, particularly if you put your hands close to his mouth. Don't worry about your dog swallowing his tongue—this is a myth.

As soon as your dog has stopped convulsing, rub a small amount of honey on his gums and tongue, particularly if he is a puppy. Hypoglycemia (low blood sugar) is a common cause of seizures (especially in puppies) and a quick but temporary "fix" is possible if you can quickly give him a form of rapidly absorbed glucose (sugar).

In all cases of seizure, take your dog to the vet immediately. Keep him warm and speak to him in a gentle, calming voice. The vet will want to know your dog's history and will be particularly interested in what he was doing prior to the seizure.

ASPCA Poison Control Center

If you think your pet has been poisoned, call your vet or the ASPCA National Animal Poison Control Center at (900) 443-0000 immediately. The charge is billed directly to the caller's phone. You can also call (888) 4ANI-HELP [(888) 426-4435]; a charge is billed to the caller's credit card only. Follow-up calls can be made for no additional charge by dialing (888) 299-2973.

Hypoglycemia

Any dog who has been refusing to eat runs the risk of becoming hypoglycemic if he avoids eating for a long enough period. The dog may appear to be weak or even blind. He may be "twitchy," and if still strong enough to walk, he will stagger. He will usually be disoriented. If the hypoglycemia is not corrected, he will progress to seizures, unconsciousness, and eventual death.

Again, if you think your dog is hypoglycemic, open his mouth and rub a small amount of honey on his gums and tongue. Do not administer liquids because he may not be able to coordinate his swallow reflex at this point and could aspirate the fluids. Honey is thick enough to prevent aspiration and is quickly absorbed through the mucous membranes of the mouth.

Take your dog to the vet and carefully describe what happened. The vet will need to do a series of tests to determine why your dog became hypoglycemic in the first place.

Hypothermia

If your dog becomes too cold, either from being exposed to inclement weather or being submerged in cold water, he will become hypothermic (body temperature dangerously low).

If hypothermic, your dog will undoubtedly be shivering and lethargic. Warm him slowly. If you warm your dog too quickly, particularly by placing very warm objects such as heating pads next to his skin, you may cause his body to react to all that heat by trying to cool him down. Instead, wrap him in blankets and hold him close to your body. You can also submerge him in a tub of warm water approximately 102°F (38.9°C). While he is submerged in the warm water, continue taking the temperature of the water and keep it at 102°F (38.9°C). Keep the room warm and be prepared to briskly towel your dog dry once he is removed from the tub, followed by blowing him dry.

Heatstroke

Because dogs don't have sweat glands in their skin, they will often utilize their natural instinct to pant to cool themselves. However, one of the signs of heatstroke is fast, loud panting. The mucous membranes of the mouth will be bright red, and the dog may walk unsteadily. A sure diagnosis can be made by taking a rectal temperature reading, remembering that the normal temperature of a dog is approximately 100°F to 102.5°F (37.8° to 38.9°C).

If your dog appears to be suffering from heatstroke, wet him down, and if possible, direct a small fan toward his dampened fur. You can submerge him in a tub of lukewarm water if you are able to do so, but the water must be only lukewarm and not icy cold. Allow your dog to slowly drink cool water as well. The object is to cool him down, but not so quickly that his temperature drops below 100°F (37.8°C).

Heatstroke Symptoms

If your Cavalier is exposed to very hot temperatures, and you see the following symptoms, it may be heatstroke:

- dazed expression
- increased heart/pulse rate
- moisture accumulating on feet
- rapid mouth breathing
- reddened gums
- thickened saliva
- vomiting

Open Wounds

A wound is an emergency if there is profuse bleeding or if it is very deep or has created an open area in the head, abdomen, or chest. After taking some precautionary measures, take to your dog to the vet as soon as possible.

Stopping the bleeding is the first thing to worry about. Using clean towels, apply pressure to the wound. If the bleeding continues and soaks through the towel, continue reinforcing the original bandage by the applying more towels on top. Do not remove the original bandage because to do so may dislodge a clot if one is forming. If possible, elevate the affected area and apply a cold pack to the tissue surrounding the wound. Tourniquets on or above extremities are to be avoided unless the bleeding simply cannot be stopped in any other way and the dog's death may occur if the bleeding continues. Be aware that by using a tourniquet you may be causing the loss of the affected limb. A better technique is to apply pressure to pressure points near the dog's limbs. Pressure points for the front legs are located inside the leg just above the elbow. For the rear legs, they are inside the thigh, where the femoral artery crosses over the thigh bone. The bone underneath the artery also provides a firm surface for the application of pressure. The pressure point for the tail is located on the underside of the base of the tail.

If your dog has a chest wound that is making a whistling or "sucking" sound, place a piece of nonporous plastic or even aluminum foil over the hole and tape it securely in place. The object of covering a wound in this manner is to make it airtight.

If your dog has an abdominal wound, place warm, wet sterile dressings over the open area. If you use saline solution to wet the dressing, you are less likely to cause pain and discomfort; when treating open wounds, saline solution is preferable to plain water.

If the wounds appear to be dirty, pour warmed saline solution directly over them to clean the area. Once you have applied the dressings, cover them with plastic wrap to keep them moist. If they start to dry out, pour more warm saline over them, especially while in transit to the vet.

Electrical Shock

Because dogs love to chew on exposed wires and cords, electrical shocks and their resulting burns are fairly common. The resulting electrical impulse may stop the heart and kill a dog instantly, but at the least it is almost certain to cause burn trauma to the interior of the mouth.

Before doing anything, you must first protect yourself. Do not touch your dog until you have made certain that the electrical plug

Your dog's overall quality of life should be the first and most important factor you consider as he advances in age.

is safely disconnected from the outlet or the power has been turned off to the house. To treat your dog for shock, keep him warm and take him immediately to the vet.

Burns

A burn injury is usually either very obvious because the skin will be charred and will smell of singed hair and burned flesh, or less obvious because the skin will look very white. Often, several layers of tissue are exposed.

First, place towels well soaked with icy water onto the burned areas. Your goal is to stop the burning and arrest damage to the soft tissue, which might continue unless the temperature of the skin drops as fast as possible. If only small areas such as the feet are burned, you can submerge them directly into cold water. This will cool the surrounding tissue and stop the burn damage from continuing. However, it is not advisable to submerge large areas of burned tissue. Instead, cover them with cold, wet towels and make every attempt to keep the area as clean as possible. Watch your dog for signs of shock, and keep him warm during transport to the vet.

THE AGING CAVALIER

Although unfair, a large number of Cavaliers die early due to MVD, but many can live to a ripe old age. Sometimes it's hard to realize that your "baby" has actually reached middle age because his nature tends to make him behave like a perpetual puppy. But if you look closely, you may find that his body is probably experiencing some of the typical signs of aging. The fur on his muzzle and around his eyes will slowly turn silver, and you may notice that he is moving more slowly and taking longer naps. His gait will eventually stiffen, and it will take him longer to get moving in the morning. Although being kept busy and active with regular exercise is important at any stage of your dog's life, it is never more important than when he is older. Your walks may be slower and you may not travel as far, but do not let his advanced years be an excuse to allow him to simply lie in the sun and sleep.

For similar reasons, this is also the time to pay special attention to your dog's weight. Some elderly dogs become very thin, while others gain weight. Discuss proper nutrition for your aging pet with your vet so that you can chose an appropriate diet to address your dog's particular needs. Many diets are available for specific

health issues, such as low-calorie diets for overweight dogs, high-calorie diets for dogs who aren't eating enough, diets designed for dogs whose kidneys are failing, and more.

As your dog ages, also be mindful of his comfort. He may not have required stairs to get up on his favorite napping spot when he was younger, but now a ramp may be very useful to him. The older dog may chill more easily and require a warmed bed. These are sold in all pet catalogues and available online from numerous companies.

THE RAINBOW BRIDGE

The time will come when you will have to bid farewell to your Cavalier. It seems so unfair that during the course of our lifetime we have to witness the passing of so many of our beloved pets, but their shorter lifespans makes it inevitable. If you are lucky, your wonderful little Cavalier companion will die peacefully in his sleep, and you will never be faced with having to make hard decisions.

If, however, your dog is afflicted with a disease that causes irreversible pain or fear, it is a kindness to consider euthanasia. By doing so, you can give your dog the gift of a release from pain and constant discomfort. Well before the time for euthanasia approaches, discuss the possibility with your vet. He will explain the options and general procedure to you. Usually, a medication will be given to gently put your dog to sleep. Although it may sound silly, discuss the possibility with your dog as well. Those of us who been around dogs all our lives know they do hear us, understand us, and find ways to comfort and communicate with us. After you have discussed euthanasia with your vet, your family, and your dog, give yourself some time to think it through carefully. Don't be surprised if the day comes when your Cavalier is able to communicate to you with those beautiful expressive eyes that his days on earth are drawing to an end and that he is ready to go. This is the very last gift that you can give him after he has given you a lifetime of unconditional love and forgiveness.

Be prepared for the grieving process that will follow. You can find many Internet sources and support groups to help you through this difficult time. The loss of a dog is often the loss of a close friend and a most faithful companion. Allow yourself time to grieve. Find comfort in the fact that you took good care of your Cavalier and that you each experienced the friendship and love of a lifetime in the companionship of one another.

Hospice Care

If your dog is terminally ill but you're not ready to let go, you may want to look into home hospice care. Some veterinary hospitals and organizations now offer this service, keeping the animals comfortable in their own homes and giving family members time to come to terms with their impending loss. If you are interested in learning more about veterinary hospice care, ask your vet or contact your closest veterinary school. The American Association of Human-Animal Bond Veterinarians (AAH-ABV) offers information on home hospice care on their website at http://aah-abv.org.

ASSOCIATIONS AND ORGANIZATIONS

BREED CLUBS

American Kennel Club (AKC)

5580 Centerview Drive

Raleigh, NC 27606

Telephone: (919) 233-9767

Fax: (919) 233-3627

E-mail: info@akc.org

www.akc.org

Canadian Kennel Club (CKC)

89 Skyway Avenue, Suite 100

Etobicoke, Ontario M9W 6R4

Telephone: (416) 675-5511

Fax: (416) 675-6506

E-mail: information@ckc.ca

www.ckc.ca

Federation Cynologique Internationale (FCI)

Secretariat General de la FCI

Place Albert 1er, 13

B – 6530 Thuin

Belqique

www.fci.be

The Kennel Club

1 Clarges Street

London

W1J 8AB

Telephone: 0870 606 6750

Fax: 0207 518 1058

www.the-kennel-club.org.uk

United Kennel Club (UKC)

100 E. Kilgore Road

Kalamazoo, MI 49002-5584

Telephone: (269) 343-9020

Fax: (269) 343-7037

E-mail: pbickell@ukcdogs.com

www.ukcdogs.com

PET SITTERS

National Association of Professional Pet Sitters

15000 Commerce Parkway, Suite C

Mt. Laurel, New Jersey 08054

Telephone: (856) 439-0324

Fax: (856) 439-0525

E-mail: napps@ahint.com

www.petsitters.org

Pet Sitters International

201 East King Street

King, NC 27021-9161

Telephone: (336) 983-9222

Fax: (336) 983-5266

E-mail: info@petsit.com

www.petsit.com

RESCUE ORGANIZATIONS AND ANIMAL WELFARE GROUPS

American Humane Association (AHA)

63 Inverness Drive East

Englewood, CO 80112

Telephone: (303) 792-9900

Fax: 792-5333

www.americanhumane.org

American Society for the Prevention of Cruelty to Animals (ASPCA)

424 E. 92nd Street

New York, NY 10128-6804

Telephone: (212) 876-7700

www.aspca.org

Royal Society for the Prevention of Cruelty to Animals (RSPCA)

Telephone: 0870 3335 999

Fax: 0870 7530 284

www.rspca.org.uk

The Humane Society of the United States (HSUS)

2100 L Street, NW

Washington DC 20037

Telephone: (202) 452-1100

www.hsus.org

SPORTS

Canine Freestyle Federation, Inc.

Secretary: Brandy Clymire

E-Mail: secretary@canine-freestyle.org

www.canine-freestyle.org

International Agility Link (IAL)

Global Administrator: Steve Drinkwater

E-mail: yunde@powerup.au

www.agilityclick.com/~ial

North American Dog Agility Council

11522 South Hwy 3

Cataldo, ID 83810

www.nadac.com

North American Flyball Association

www.flyball.org

1400 West Devon Avenue #512

Chicago, IL 6066

800-318-6312

United States Dog Agility Association

P.O. Box 850955

Richardson, TX 75085-0955

Telephone: (972) 487-2200

www.usdaa.com

World Canine Freestyle Organization

P.O. Box 350122

Brooklyn, NY 11235-2525

Telephone: (718) 332-8336

www.worldcaninefreestyle.org

THERAPY

Delta Society

875 124th Ave NE, Suite 101

Bellevue, WA 98005

Telephone: (425) 226-7357

Fax: (425) 235-1076

E-mail: info@deltasociety.org

www.deltasociety.org

Therapy Dogs Incorporated

PO Box 5868

Cheyenne, WY 82003

Telephone: (877) 843-7364

E-mail: therdog@sisna.com

www.therapydogs.com

Therapy Dogs International (TDI)

88 Bartley Road

Flanders, NJ 07836

Telephone: (973) 252-9800

Fax: (973) 252-7171

E-mail: tdi@gti.net

www.tdi-dog.org

TRAINING

Association of Pet Dog Trainers (APDT)

150 Executive Center Drive Box 35

Greenville, SC 29615

Telephone: (800) PET-DOGS

Fax: (864) 331-0767

E-mail: information@apdt.com

www.apdt.com

National Association of Dog Obedience Instructors (NADOI)

PMB 369

729 Grapevine Hwy.

Hurst, TX 76054-2085

www.nadoi.org

VETERINARY AND HEALTH RESOURCES

Academy of Veterinary Homeopathy (AVH)

P.O. Box 9280

Wilmington, DE 19809

Telephone: (866) 652-1590

Fax: (866) 652-1590

E-mail: office@TheAVH.org

www.theavh.org

American Academy of Veterinary Acupuncture (AAVA)

100 Roscommon Drive, Suite 320

Middletown, CT 06457

Telephone: (860) 635-6300

Fax: (860) 635-6400

E-mail: office@aava.org

www.aava.org

American Animal Hospital Association (AAHA)

P.O. Box 150899

Denver, CO 80215-0899

Telephone: (303) 986-2800

Fax: (303) 986-1700

E-mail: info@aahanet.org

www.aahanet.org/index.cfm

American College of Veterinary Internal Medicine (ACVIM)

1997 Wadsworth Blvd., Suite A

Lakewood, CO 80214-5293

Telephone: (800) 245-9081

Fax: (303) 231-0880

Email: ACVIM@ACVIM.org

www.acvim.org

American College of Veterinary Ophthalmologists (ACVO)

P.O. Box 1311

Meridian, Idaho 83860

Telephone: (208) 466-7624

Fax: (208) 466-7693

E-mail: office@acvo.com

www.acvo.com

American Holistic Veterinary Medical Association (AHVMA)

2218 Old Emmorton Road

Bel Air, MD 21015

Telephone: (410) 569-0795

Fax: (410) 569-2346

E-mail: office@ahvma.org

www.ahvma.org

American Veterinary Medical Association (AVMA)

1931 North Meacham Road – Suite 100

Schaumburg, IL 60173

Telephone: (847) 925-8070

Fax: (847) 925-1329

E-mail: avmainfo@avma.org

www.avma.org

ASPCA Animal Poison Control Center

1717 South Philo Road, Suite 36

Urbana, IL 61802

Telephone: (888) 426-4435

www.aspca.org

British Veterinary Association (BVA)

7 Mansfield Street

London

W1G 9NQ

Telephone: 020 7636 6541

Fax: 020 7436 2970

E-mail: bvahq@bva.co.uk

www.bva.co.uk

Canine Eye Registration Foundation (CERF)

VMDB/CERF

1248 Lynn Hall

625 Harrison St.

Purdue University

West Lafayette, IN 47907-2026

Telephone: (765) 494-8179

E-mail: CERF@vmbd.org

www.vmdb.org

Orthopedic Foundation for Animals (OFA)

2300 NE Nifong Blvd

Columbus, Missouri 65201-3856

Telephone: (573) 442-0418

Fax: (573) 875-5073

Email: ofa@offa.org

www.offa.org

PUBLICATIONS

BOOKS

Anderson, Teoti. *The Super Simple Guide to Housetraining*. Neptune City: TFH Publications, 2004.

Morgan, Diane. *Good Dogkeeping*. Neptune City: TFH Publications, 2005.

MAGAZINES

AKC *Family Dog*

American Kennel Club

260 Madison Avenue

New York, NY 10016

Telephone: (800) 490-5675

E-mail: familydog@akc.org

www.akc.org/pubs/familydog

AKC *Gazette*

American Kennel Club

260 Madison Avenue

New York, NY 10016

Telephone: (800) 533-7323

E-mail: gazette@akc.org

www.akc.org/pubs/gazette

Dog & Kennel

Pet Publishing, Inc.

7-L Dundas Circle

Greensboro, NC 27407

Telephone: (336) 292-4272

Fax: (336) 292-4272

E-mail: info@petpublishing.com

www.dogandkennel.com

Dog Fancy

Subscription Department

P.O. Box 53264

Boulder, CO 80322-3264

Telephone: (800) 365-4421

E-mail: barkback@dogfancy.com

www.dogfancy.com

Dogs Monthly

Ascot House

High Street, Ascot,

Berkshire SL5 7JG

United Kingdom

Telephone: 0870 730 8433

Fax: 0870 730 8431

E-mail: admin@rtc-associates.freeserve.co.uk

www.corsini.co.uk/dogsmonthly

INDEX

Note: **Boldfaced** numbers indicate illustrations.

ABOUT THE AUTHOR

Myra Savant-Harris is a well-known author and educator. An RN in Labor-Delivery and Neonatal Intensive Care, Myra applied her experience in human reproductive health care to canine reproductive health care to develop a safe canine breeding program. Her books, *Canine Reproduction and Whelping* and *Puppy Intensive Care* are sold worldwide, and her seminars are in demand throughout the US and Canada.

Also a breeder of Cavalier King Charles Spaniels, Myra has studied dogs and canine behavior since childhood. She adored all of her childhood pets but it was not until she owned her first Cavalier that she fell completely in love with the breed. She has said that Cavaliers taught her how to communicate with her dogs and how to listen when they communicated with her. Her stud dog, Ch. Peakdowns Aidan, has ranked among the top ten producers in the breed since he was two years old and has sired many AKC and CKCSC champions.

Myra lives in Washington state with her husband, Doug, and enjoys time spent with her dogs, her 10 adult children, and every single one of her 36 grandchildren.

Nylabone® Cares.

Millions of dogs of all ages, breeds, and sizes have enjoyed our world-famous chew bones—but we're not just bones! Nylabone®, the leader in responsible animal care for over 50 years, devotes the same care and attention to our many other award-winning, high-quality innovative products. Your dog will love them — and so will you!

Toys　　　Treats　　　Chews　　　Crates　　　Grooming

Available at retailers everywhere. Visit us online at www.nylabone.com